The Proof of the Pudding

The Proof of the Pudding:

WHAT CHILDREN READ

Phyllis Fenner

THE JOHN DAY COMPANY NEW YORK

Published by The John Day Company, 62 West 45th Street, New York 36, N. Y., and on the same day in Canada by Longmans, Green & Company, Toronto.

Library of Congress Catalog
Card Number: 57:5981

MANUFACTURED IN THE UNITED STATES OF AMERICA

For
Walter and Margaret Hard
of The Johnny Appleseed Bookshop
with affection and admiration

Contents

Introduction

THIS IS A BOOK for the fathers and mothers and grandparents who want to, and should, buy and borrow books for their children. Also, it is for the proverbial maiden aunt who usually buys the wrong book for the right child. It is so difficult to know, with all the books today, what book appeals to a child. It is hard to remember what we liked, or how old we were when we liked it. The so-called classics of yesterday are not, as a rule, the books with which to start a child off. They are good for building up his library, but who wants to wait years to read? Also, there are many "new classics" since grandpa was a boy, and it has been twenty years, at least, since father read the books he thinks his ten-year-old boy would like.

This is not a history of children's literature. It is not advice on what they ought to read, nor is it even about the best literature you can find. It does not pretend to be about *all* of the books that will interest children. Simply, it is about some of the best-liked books of all times, telling you a little about them, why a child likes them, and approximately how old a child is when he reads them.

As we know, every child is an individual, and naturally there will be some variation with different children. The books mentioned here are suggestions. Many others of like subject and caliber might have been put in. This is a starting point. It will introduce you to some popular authors, suggest some things to read aloud, and in some instances, tell you the best-liked editions of books.

At the end you will find two essays on children's books and reading, one by Padraic Colum, "Imagination and Children's Literature"; the other by Henry Barnes, "The Wingèd Horse: An Essay on the Art of Reading." They have helped me in my work with children. You will find them beautiful and inspiring.

The children themselves won't need to read this book. They *know* what they want.

P. F.

The Proof of the Pudding

I

"The proof of the pudding is in the eating."

BRINGING CHILDREN AND BOOKS TOGETHER

I WAS WALKING along the corridor one morning when I met a rather glum-looking little snow-suited figure. "Hello, Jack," I called cheerily. "How's your mother? You know, you have a wonderful mother." "One man's opinion," he replied grumpily.

What I have to say is strictly one woman's opinion, but it is backed up by thirty-two years of working with children, two generations of them. I am not going to talk about why children "don't read," or *how* they read, but *what* they read. For, as most of us who have worked with children for a long time know, not only do more children read today, but they read better—and many more—books than children did a generation ago.

Not so many years ago we had lots of children who didn't read at all. They knew how, but as one little girl said "I get enough reading in school." The trouble was, we had no books for some children. Many children do not like "made-up stories." They want to read about true things—people, science, history, and "how to do it" books. Up to a few years ago we had none to speak of. There were no children's books that answered the little girl's question, "Do squirrels come from eggs?" or, "How does a grasshopper swallow?" or "What makes color in birds' feathers?" We adults, if we knew the answers, answered their questions. If we didn't, we evaded. Now we send children to books to find their own answers. Now we have many wonderful books on almost every subject, to suit any taste, and even books, like The True Books Series, that the very youngest reader can read himself.

We have learned a great deal about children, too. We know they are interested in everything around them. We realize that, just like us superior grownups, they have individual tastes, they don't all like the same things. Nor will they all love to read as a pastime. It would be a pretty poor world to live in if all people were bookworms. Where would we get our radio sets or modern gadgets, or anything, if it were not for those who prefer to work with their hands?

Marshall's mother was terribly upset because he did not read story books all the time. Once when he was sick she took three books home for him. She called me in great excitement the next morning. "I think we have him started," she said. But when he came back to school he had no time to read, for Marshall was making radio sets for every kid on his street. He read great big radio books but he had no time for stories . . . unless he was sick.

Bob won a trip to California for himself and his mother when he was nine by inventing an electric ditchdigger to go with his Erektor set. He never read more than he could help. As his mother said, "He wouldn't have bothered to learn to read if he hadn't had to know what it said under the electrical diagrams in the books on electricity." Almost every week his mother was in to see if we couldn't get Bob to read *Robin Hood* or some of the books the other boys were reading. Bob tried to co-operate pleasantly but he wasn't really interested. A few years ago he graduated from M.I.T. He came in to see me. "Well, Miss Fenner," he said, stretching out his long legs as he sat in one of my little library chairs, "I don't read much more than I used to. I read the

Reader's Digest now and then. My handwriting is just as bad as it was but I have a typewriter." We who love to read, love words and book people, feel badly to have children miss our favorites and to miss the joy we know from reading. But obviously we can't all do everything. Some of us have to be the doers and some the readers.

There are so many wonderful books and so many bright, eager children, it would be wonderful if we could bring them together. And we should try. Sometimes the child who isn't reading is a potential booklover, and we should try to show him the joys of reading. But often he is like the Bobs and Marshalls.

Why do we want children to read? It is more than that we feel they should know about other peoples and other ideas. Knowing the world's great books is like knowing a common language. We say, "I won't be your Man Friday," or "She was a Cinderella," or "Don't kill the goose that laid the golden egg," and those of us who know the old tales know what is meant. I was going through the gate with the electric eye in Pennsylvania Station. Right behind me was a gang of rough street boys. As they went through with a rush they shouted "Open Sesame!" I admit to getting a great satisfaction from their knowing "Ali Baba and the Forty Thieves."

We have a feeling, too, that children are not booklovers if they are not reading fiction. Also, we expect them all to read the things we know are good, like *The Story of Doctor Dolittle, Mary Poppins, Heidi.* We grownups do not all enjoy the same sort of books.

If we want these practical children to read we must approach them through their interests. Hobart would not read a book if he could help it until, one day, coming to the library for some snake pictures, he discovered that there were many books on snakes. It was fun leading him on. From snake books he read the life of Ditmars, and Roy Chapman Andrews. Then he went on to nature books and finally even to stories with a nature background. I would not say that

Hobart ever became a booklover. He was a very specialized reader. But he did read a great deal.

There are many things we can do to bring children and books together, and we shall talk about some of them. But as Anne Eaton says in her truly great book *Reading With Children,** "It is not a simple task. It means knowing children and knowing books so thoroughly that we may help the dreamer see the wonder and romance of the world around him, and the matter of fact child to enter the realm of imaginative literature . . . We must have retained or we must recapture for ourselves something of the child's own attitude toward life and the world."

* Eaton, Anne Thaxter, *Reading with Children,* Viking, p. 38.

II

"The children haven't changed."

WHAT CHILDREN LIKE

TWO LITTLE GIRLS were walking along a dusty mountain road in one of the Maristan Chapman mysteries. Suddenly, one of them exclaimed: "I'm so full of pentupness I could scream." That is the way I feel when I think of children and books. Children are thrilling with all their frankness, their eagerness and freshness of outlook. Books are thrilling with their words and vitality and satisfyingness. Bringing the two together is one of the most exciting things I know.

What are children like? We used to think they were all alike. Some people think children have changed. How many times do we hear: "We weren't like that when we were their age." *But the children haven't changed!* We can tell the very seasons by children, year after year. When a story hour is interrupted by marbles rolling out of little boys' pockets I know beyond a doubt that spring has arrived. When my little neighbor, Frankie, stops by with his bathing suit wrapped in a Turkish towel, a peanut-butter sandwich in his hand, I know that summer is here, for haven't little boys, for years and years, been doing the same thing, even to eating the same kind of sandwich? Then comes a day when on the school ground I see little figures in big football helmets, hot and sweaty, tustling and tackling each other, and I know the leaves will be dropping soon, and cold weather is on its way. Some weeks later I go into the Principal's office. There on a bench sit some sad-looking boys. They have been caught throwing snowballs on the school grounds. The boys are different but it's the same old trouble.

No, the children haven't changed—unless they are quicker on the uptake than they used to be. We have changed, however. We are older, less resilient, more conservative. We are forgetful. We are less tolerant. We think that what we used to read was the best. How long has it been since we were in the fifth grade? We have forgotten the process of learning to read. We have forgotten at what age we read what. The mother who left *Tom Sawyer* around hoping her eight-year-old boy would pick it up had forgotten that she herself most probably was a lot older than that when she read it. Time has a way of telescoping itself.

What do these children have, what qualities that remain forever the same, generation in and generation out?

They have a terrible honesty, for one thing. Their minds are not cluttered up with crooked thoughts. Said Ruth Sawyer, that wonderful storyteller and author, when someone criticized her Newbery Prize book *Roller Skates* because she had mentioned the word murder in it, "We confront children with our own lack of Faith. To safeguard them we attempt to thrust between them and life those many false illusions which we may have picked up in our own twisting, turning way. Children make a far more direct approach if we will let them." "I don't like to read," says the boy. And he means it. "This book is dull," says the little girl. And it probably is.

Do you remember the wonderful chapter in Jessamyn West's *Friendly Persuasion,* where Jess, the old man, makes friends with the young boy, Homer? He wondered why he got such pleasure from the friendship:

> The pleasure comes from two things, he thought. It comes from seeing, once again, what we started with and lost. Honesty, he

guessed, would come as near as any word to saying what it was. Wonder, fear, love, there it all was in Homer, nothing glossed over, nothing hidden from sight. It was meeting a human being at first hand, not as was the case with most grownups, second hand, if at all; not meeting a person assembled, put together so's to present to the inspecting eye the very object for which it was searching. Ah, Jess thought, after eighty years, thee gets tired of peering through the chinks and knotholes trying to catch sight of something alive inside the makeshift building. It's a pleasure to see something all of one piece, alive, clear to the outside.

It is hard to put ourselves back into the child's world. His likes and dislikes, his fears and foolishnesses, are of an entirely different sort from ours. The humor of the child is amazing. Few of us can remember back to the things that struck us as funny. What nonsense, these stupid jokes they play! How foolish we think are the things they laugh at. Once I read a manuscript to a group of eight-year-olds. It was later put into a beautiful little book called *Pinky Finds a Home.* It was the story of a toy rabbit, thrown onto a dump heap in the desert. The children lost their breath with laughter when Pinky stubbed his toe on a hamburger. To me it didn't seem funny at all. And some things that seem funny to us are not funny to them. My little niece wept over Doctor Dolittle. "He was such a brave man," she sobbed. When I tried to give Bill an *Augustus* book to read, because it was funny, he said with great dignity, "I don't like funny books. I like serious books like *Freddy the Detective.*"

It is difficult for us to remember—oh, so difficult!

Children are loyal to friends and book friends. A seventh grade was in the library telling me about books they had read. The chairman called for volunteers. Jim, a slow-speaking boy, spoke up: "I have just been reading a book called *Iron Duke,* by John R. Tunis." He told about it. The chairman waited for another volunteer. Finally, Jim slowly began again, "There's another book I have just been reading. It is called *Duke Decides,* by John R. Tunis." The chairman waited. Then Jim started in again. "There is another book I just read. It is called *Champion's Choice.* It is about girls, and I don't like girls. It is about tennis, and I don't like tennis. But it is by my favorite author, John R. Tunis, so I read it, and I liked it." An extreme case of loyalty!

"Sol-ID. Mel-LOW. Neat!" The expressions change with the styles but the enthusiasm is the same. For that is one of the great qualities of children. "Enthusiasm—an eagerness to share something we dearly love with someone else who will love it,—there is nothing in the world so persuasive and powerful."* A person with enthusiasm can "sell" anything. The teacher in my school who loved poetry created a love of it in her pupils, one they will always have. The teacher who loved *The Iliad* and *The Odyssey* made her children so excited over Colum's *Children's Homer* that they took sides in the battles. The mother who loved E. Nesbit's *Bastable Children* gave her boy and girl a love for it that will go on to their children. Enthusiasm! If we all only had more of it, for life, for people, for books, we would be better parents, better teachers, better people.

Children are intensely curious. An exaggerated example of that was Toady. He was a beautiful little boy with sort of cocoa-colored hair and splotchy freckles. I have never known such a child. Before he could read to himself he took books home for his mother to read to him. He pursued one interest very hard, and then, suddenly, overnight it seemed, he was off on another track. Books about Ireland he demanded, all kinds of books—folk tales, true stories, geography. Then suddenly, it was cave men Toady wanted. Finally, he wanted to know about Presidents. It was difficult to find lives of Presidents for such a little fellow. I asked him, "Toady, why do you want to read about them?" "I might want to be one someday," he replied, "and I think I ought to know what they are like." Then he wanted books on the army, the navy, and finally, one bitter cold day, I met him

* Anne Thaxter Eaton, *Reading with Children,* Viking.

at the railroad station. "Going some place?" I inquired. "Just watching the trains," he replied. "You can learn an awful lot watching trains." Then, as if he read my mind, he smiled and said, "I think this is going to last." Some weeks later, at our library book sale, his mother ordered a book on chess for Toady. "Oh, dear!" she said as she was leaving, "I hope he is still interested in chess at Christmas."

Children pursue interests *hard,* and then drop them just as fast. Billy spent hours after school looking up about the ships that fought in the Coral Sea. Why? No one knows. David goes from one thing to another. One day: "Do you have a book that shows how to pack a pack horse for camping?" Another day it is medieval weapons he is interested in. The same with girls. Stories about one thing, family, mystery, horse, until you'd think the saturation point had been reached. Eventually it is, and then some other subject is overworked. Overworked, that is, from a grownup's point of view. Probably more parents worry over this trait in their children than any other. "He reads nothing but sea stories" is a common complaint. Or, "nothing but horse stories." The thing that bothers most of us about our children is that we think they have these little traits all by themselves, no other child has them. The truth is, most of them actually go through a pattern. It is a comfort, I think, to know this. And most of them come out fine. It takes great subtlety to get a child off a subject he isn't ready to leave. The girl who reads nothing but horse stories—and it is mostly girls who read about horses—will read *The Good Master* or *Cinders* because in those stories the children ride horseback a great deal, but in reading them, she is getting much more than a horse story, there is another kind of adventure and there is characterization and beauty.

Children are real individuals. Fortunate it is that they do not all like the same things. We grownups would like to have them all alike, I sometimes believe. We expect them to like the books we think are worth while. We don't expect all grownups to like the same things. Children, unlike grownups, do not read books because they are best sellers or much talked about. They read nothing but what interests them. What the other fellow thinks doesn't matter. Too, children do not read things because they think they should. "It's dull," "Not enough adventures," "Slow beginning," they comment. Or in spite of grownups saying that certain books are not good, the girls still say, "But I like Nancy Drew." And there ends the argument. In which case, we must just patiently bide our time until the children find out for themselves that certain books are not worth their efforts.

Children love to sound like grownups. "What I want is a good murder mystery," says the seven-year-old. He doesn't really know what it is. They often choose books way beyond them because they have the desire to read big things, and usually that means that eventually they will achieve it.

Lucky it is that children are different, one from another. Lucky for people who publish books. Lucky for librarians who provide them. Lucky for parents, too.

It must be wonderful to be at the age when one can be really independent. Children don't care how famous an author is. They are frank and honest in expressing their opinions of an author as if the world had never heard of him. "Too much talk for what happened," said Bob about a manuscript I had read his class for criticism. He was right, too. How many of us grownups dare say we don't like a very popular book of the moment, or more still, a book the world has proclaimed great?

Their interests are varied. One child is reading about the South Sea Islands, another about baseball, another a family story, another a book on radio. Girls of ten years, and up, are more likely to want to read the popular girls' books, probably not for the same reason grownups read popular books, because they are much talked of, but because the books are really interesting to girls of their age.

Age seems to dull our imaginations. Some seven-year-olds were playing *The Tale of Peter Rabbit.* They all wanted to be either Peter or Mr. McGregor. And who can blame them since they were the only two important characters? Scarcely knowing what to do in all the hubbub, I called one little boy to me. "See here," I said, "you can't all be Peter or Mr. McGregor. Take something else and make it important." Without a minute's hesitation, he replied, "I'll be the watering can." My imagination could never have conjured up anything so entrancing! When a group was playing *Jack and the Beanstalk* and we were choosing parts, some of the children wanted to be the beans. They were, and they actually *grew* before my eyes, gracefully, into a beanstalk, and later Jack cut them down. Padraic Colum in his article "Imagination and Children's Literature" says: "Imagination is the faculty of revealing things freshly and surprisingly. . . ."

III

"You wouldn't know hardly anything if there wasn't books."

WHAT BOOKS CAN DO FOR US

WE WHO LOVE BOOKS think there is nothing quite so wonderful. To use the old cliché, they are meat and drink to us.

There are some of us grownups who love them just for the information in them. We can put them flat on their faces and crack the bindings; even tear out a page now and then. Some like to read the popular books so they can discuss them. The bindings, decorations and type mean nothing at all. For such, the paperbacks are a godsend. There are others who collect rare books and first editions, caring nothing much for what is inside. Others want them to fill up shelves. Witness the woman, and not so long ago, who called her book dealer to ask for one hundred books in fine bindings. She didn't care what they were about as long as the colors were right in her room.

But there are some of us who not only love the outsides and lovely print, spacious margins and illustrations, but we also treasure and trace lovingly the words written within. We love the *whole* book. Some children have that feeling too. Wrote Cynthia, "I think everyone should read *Shadow In The Pines*. It's just packed with adventure. But this is not like all books. Have you ever read a book and wondered when the mystery will come? Well, here the people are interesting along with the mystery. So when there is no mystery it is packed with fun where they live in the woods. One of the things I liked most about this book is the way it is *printed. It is nice and roomy and has an interesting picture* in the beginning of every chapter. The author is Stephen Meader who has written other books also. . . ."

Children like books for almost as many reasons as there are different kinds of children. Some like them, or perhaps like a single book, because it meant something particular at a particular time. John, who had been having trouble with his reading, found *Kit and Kat* as simple a story as you could find. "Kit was a boy. Kat was a girl. Kit and Kat were twins." He was impressed. "How can such a big book be so easy?" he exclaimed, with real reverence. The first book he could read! Will he ever forget it?

The children haven't changed. Books haven't changed, either, *in what they can do for us*. There are more books for children, many more. There are more good books and more mediocre books too. It is more difficult to select. No longer can we go into a library or book shop and just ask for the good old books. We have before us hundreds of very good-looking books on every subject. Thirty years ago there were few books for children except the old ones. There were very few books on other countries, science, history or poetry. Now there are many—easy to read, too. And they are being published every day, on all subjects, from snakes to atoms. And the children read them. I was impressed by the times in which we live when a group of first graders made their first trip to the library at the opening of school. Over half of those six-year-olds wanted books about snakes instead of the regular picture books.

What is it that books can do for children, for any of us? There is real magic in them for some children. They carry them off to other worlds, other places, other people, other times.

There is no frigate like a book
To take us lands away,
Nor any coursers like a page
Of prancing poetry.

wrote Emily Dickinson.

For books are more than books, they are the life
The very heart and core of ages past,
The reason why men lived and worked and died,
The essence and quintessence of their lives.

wrote Amy Lowell.

With Mrs. Wilder's family in *The Little House in the Big Woods* children live in an earlier day, through winter cold, prairie fires, Indians and log cabins. With *Nuvat the Brave* they experience danger, cold and loneliness. With Captain Nemo in *Twenty Thousand Leagues Under the Sea* they visit the strange world under the water. With Kate in *The Good Master* they ride on the Hungarian plains. With Edison they discover the possibilities of electricity. With Andrews they explore the Gobi Desert.

Three girls were walking down a hot suburban street with their arms over each other's shoulders chanting, "All for one and one for all." They were the musketeers, far away from their immediate surroundings. Even children these days need vicarious adventure.

Swiss Family Robinson takes children on very exciting adventures with shipwrecks and desert islands. Even though, as one boy said, "It has a few too many items in it," it is an extremely popular book today.

Johnny Tremain makes real the dangers of living during the American Revolution. As Billy wrote about it, "I wish it were two hundred pages longer."

Silk and Satin Lane brings little girls right into the family life of a little Chinese girl. And there is no break with today when they read *Ojibway Drums* or *The Ordeal of the Young Hunter,* so real are they.

With *Little Tim and the Brave Sea Captain* very young children have brave adventures, as if they themselves were right there with little Tim.

Mysteries bring a little suspense into the everyday living of today in which there is too much regulation of activities. "I like mysteries because they are so sus*pense*ful," wrote a boy.

Books stretch children's imaginations. The old folk tales with seven league boots, magic runes, and strange creatures like trolls, giants, wee red men, with magic power, are right up a child's alley. He *knows* there is magic. When I had told the story of "The Stolen Turnips" to a four-year-old and his mother said to him afterwards, "Maybe *our* table cloths are magic too," Stephen replied, "Oh no! I tried them." The magic of today in flights to mushroom planets in the marvels of modern inventions, stretches children's understanding and curiosity.

Humor in books not only amuses but it brings people together. As the little girl said in a story, "People laugh in the same language." Children who are not readers like funny stories. There is nothing like humor to unite a group. The way people laugh at themselves, at each other, is revealing. Children love to laugh. *Mr. Popper's Penguins, Don't Blame Me, Not Really, The Three Policemen, The Peterkin Papers,* will interest all children, and perhaps lead those who have not yet found the joy in books to the realization of what they can mean.

Books give us words, beautiful words. Some children love them and savor them. The words in stories help a child's speaking vocabulary, teach him new meanings in reading. "Youth," the seven-year-old girl corrected me politely, when I used the word "boy" in a story. The tiny girl who demanded *Mary Poppins* so many times used some expressions from the book. "I'll thank you to do so and so," she would say pertly. Warren, who loved *King Arthur* and other stories of knights, was heard in his back yard shouting to the boys:

"Get the hell out of here or I'll rend thee asunder." Yes, children love words and good books use good words. Sandra would not have learned to read had it not been for the books of beauty like *In My Mother's House, Wonderclock,* and *Cinders.* She would stop long over a word and say dreamily, "What a beautiful word," or "What a lovely [word] picture."

The practical child will love books for what they give him. "This is my favorite book," said the boy about *Harper's Book of Electricity.* "It tells me what I want to know." Some children are born "researchers." They are continually looking up things. One boy stayed night after night to use the encyclopedia to find out, if he could, what made color in birds' feathers.

Books give children something to think about. They "make your mind a pleasant place in which to spend your leisure." An educator twenty years ago said that today's children wouldn't be able to stand boredom. Reading gives them things to think about when sitting quietly, traveling, having time on their hands.

Most children are sentimental. At a certain period in their lives, little girls particularly like to weep. Books give them an outlet. "It is the saddest and the best book I ever read," said the girl about *A Tree For Peter.* "This is practically the best book I ever read," sobbed the eight-year-old as she was reading Andersen's Fairy Tales.

Books teach children tolerance—tolerance of other kinds of peoples, other customs, other ideas. Children like to read about other children with problems, too. It is good to know that other people have problems. It helps us in ours. Parents and teachers find that they can bring to children the results of thoughtlessness, cruelty, unfairness, through books. "What book have you that will help me show the children that some of the things they do on the playground are cruel?" asked a teacher. *The Hundred Dresses* served that purpose. The children loved the story, and the lesson went home in a way that could never have been by direct talking about the problem.

Books broaden children's interests. They tell them about things they never knew could be: activities, different kinds of peoples, different occupations, different creatures. It is interesting to watch children go through the same phases at the same ages. Such as an interest in jokes. They follow you around to read you a riddle or a funny story. They are much better shared, of course.

Books are a common language the whole world over. Book friends we have in common. Quotations, expressions, thoughts, can be shared by children all over the world. A Ulysses can mean but one thing, a wanderer. Everyone knows what a Cinderella maid is, a Galahad, a Robin Hood. "I won't be your Man Friday" can mean but one thing—"I won't do your dirty work." Your "Achilles heel" is your vulnerable spot.

Children love old stories, the ones their parents talk about. Through the old stories there is continuity, a sense of security of things that have "stayed put." In these messy times children need something to hang on to, something that has had roots for a long time. "Why are you reading that?" asked a big girl of her little sister, "You know it by heart." "That's why I like it," replied the child calmly.

The omnivorous reader is interesting to watch. Jack reads every kind of thing. He is always reading a book, sometimes a sea mystery, sometimes a funny book, sometimes an animal story. On the other hand, some children are naturally choosy. They do not seem to read much but their instinct is for the special, the excellent, the lovely thing. John always picked with care. He just naturally liked *The Wind In the Willows* and wished there were more like it. Carol just naturally liked *Roller Skates* and *The Little Prince*. So many times parents have said to me that their children didn't read, and yet, when I talked with the children they were very well informed, not only about things, but about books. We are inclined to think a child has not read a great deal if he has not read the books *we* know. Think of the quantities of good books that have been published since our childhood! We are the ignorant ones, not they.

Many children go through phases. "Oh, dear!" sighs the mother, "she reads nothing but horse stories." Or, "nothing but mysteries." Can the mother but be patient, the daughter will switch to something else just as hard, or can be subtly led to something else, and then go on with that something just as strenuously. It is really strange, and there must be some purpose in it, that we forget what we ourselves were like. As I look back, I realize I exhausted a subject pretty thoroughly. I remember reading twenty-seven volumes of *Frontier Boys.* And I can still smell the bacon and beans cooking over the campfire in the desert. Worthless books they were, I am sure, yet they must have given me something because I remember them so vividly.

Some children like best the pictures in books; not because they can't read, but they naturally like illustrations. Joan's mother worried because Joan, a big girl, brought home picture books. Years later I asked about Joan. The mother smiled happily, "Oh, Joan is fine. She is studying art now." Joan had a reason to like pictures.

Children like quiet books, too, books that give them peace and contentment and an inner satisfaction. Cozy books. Little children want *Goodnight Moon* to go to bed by. They love little nature things like *All The Year Round.*

Yes, children love books for many reasons, and books give them very much. Whether the worry over the comics has subsided or whether parents have called it a losing fight, I don't know. Or perhaps television has taken the place in their worries. I do know that many very bright children, good readers, like comics. I must admit I can't see why myself, but we know it is true. Banning them has not proved effective. What a child can't read at home he can get at the neighbors. Some people have tried rationing the number of comics or television programs. The children who read books are not in much danger from either. The danger is for the child who never reads and gets all of his ideas from comics. We grownups are very often at fault. We might look at our own activities. We are all tending to take short cuts in reading and "spectator sports." Look at the number of "digests" on the market. Not only do magazines digest other magazine articles but some publishers have abridged their own books. Pill form is the trend today. Get it fast and easy. Pictures, not words, are popular. Get your news at a glance. How can we expect children to be different from ourselves? Several years ago I gave a beautiful book I had enjoyed to a friend to read. He came rushing in with it. "I could put this whole book in one paragraph" he said. "But why would you want to?" I asked him. He looked puzzled and rushed off again. Why put everything into capsules? Words are fun and beautiful and meaningful.

Parents who are concerned should look around and take stock themselves. If children never read books, perhaps parents can help by reading to them. Both would enjoy them. There are plenty of fascinating books for children that adults would enjoy too. They have enough humor, philosophy and wisdom to satisfy adults. Begin with funny stories, tall tales, folklore. Once the children get a taste for stories they are on their way to better things, and the comics and television will take their proper places in the scheme.

Someone has said that children too, need to relax these days. And it is no more peculiar for them to sprawl on the floor with *Famous Funnies* before starting homework than for father to read Agatha Christie after his day's work. When a mother worries because her athlete son has reading difficulties, she doesn't remember that neither she nor her husband reads anything but the newspaper. No books scattered invitingly around the living room—no wonder the young athlete is a radio fan.

But going back to us who really want to bring children

and books together. We see all these beautiful books for children. We read the reviews of some twelve hundred that come out each year. We are told how excellent they are, the ones that receive prizes, the ones children shouldn't miss. We know all the bright, eager children, or grandchildren, nieces, friends. We yearn to have the children read these lovely books. We forget what it is like to be a child, that children are individuals too. It would be nice if all these lovely children loved the lovely books. Life would be simple. But they don't! I think maybe we should be grateful that children *are* different, that some like fairy tales and some like books about snakes. The publishers should be grateful, too. Wouldn't life be a bore if everyone liked just what we like?

"What the boy chiefly dabbled in was natural history and fairy tales, and he just took them as they came, in a sandwichy sort of way, without making any distinctions; and really, his course of reading strikes one as rather sensible."*

* *The Reluctant Dragon.* Kenneth Grahame.

IV

"Of course, you haven't had my background."

THE NEED OF BACKGROUND FOR READING

"HERE IS A SCRAP of leather," said the art teacher to the little girl. "Why don't you make a book mark for your father?"

"He doesn't read," answered the little girl.

"Doesn't he know how?" the teacher asked facetiously.

"I don't know. I never saw him," the little girl replied very seriously.

The blindness of grownups amazes me. We have forgotten more about childhood than we remember. How many times do parents say, "Bob just can't do arithmetic. But then, Aunt Helen never could either." Or, "Mary can't sing a note, but you know her father is a monotone." Did you ever hear anyone say: "John doesn't read. Of course, his mother never cracks a book"? And yet, why not? The parent's reading habits, the talk that goes on in the home, the books that surround them, play a big, big part in whether a child loves to read, or even learns to read, for that matter. I remember reading some place that agitated parents who seek advice because Sammy never reads anything ever, and doesn't like to read, are in most cases nonreaders themselves. "They are in the same club as the mother who drove her children to Sunday School wearing a coat over her nightgown and the father who talked sports without ever having played anything himself." We are strange people, we adults. Poor memories. Poor reasoning. Poor imagination. Just *poor,* I guess.

I once took a sixth grade into New York to see Richard II when Maurice Evans was playing in it. I had seen it a couple of times and loved it. Our sixth graders were studying the Middle Ages at the time. "What a wonderful picture of the Middle Ages," I thought, "with the costumes, the jousting, and all the rest." I hadn't thought it possible to take the whole group, some thirty-five of them, but I had thought possibly I could take three or four girls who were serious and interested. When I went to our principal with my idea she said very emphatically, "Oh no. You can't do that, just ask two or three." Then she brightened. "I know what you can do," she said. "Invite the whole class. They won't all want to go but the three or four who are really interested will, and that will make it all right." I must have done a good selling job because the *whole* class voted, as a man, to go. I was in a bit of a dither but the die was cast. I was in for it. The teacher and I began to do a thorough job of preparing those kids, some of them most unliterary or unserious. We had the illustrated booklet of the play. We talked about the actors, about the characters in the play, the story; even read some of it. The day came. The children were impressed. We had a whole car on the Long Island Rail Road with our name, Manhasset Public School, tacked on it. There must have been sixty of us, including some parents. The Pennsylvania Railroad had detectives meet us at the train to escort us through the station (not to protect *us,* I am sure). It all went through without a hitch. We lost no children. No damage was done. The children really did enjoy it; even those not interested in literature were thrilled by the drama, and our electricity experts were thrilled with the stage lighting and other mechanical things. We had done a thorough job, apparently. As we were standing outside the theater waiting to go in, one of our boys saw Augustus Duncan, the blind actor, being led in. "There goes John of Gaunt!" he shouted. It was a completely successful performance, and worth all the sleep I had lost the night before. A couple of weeks later, Molly's parents went to see the play. When they returned late at night they went in to see if Molly was asleep. Sleepily Molly asked, "Did you like the play?" Her mother said, "Yes, but I must admit there were some things I didn't understand." *"Of course, you didn't have my background,"* said Molly. Molly's mother, from Vassar, and her father, from Groton and Yale, mentally rolled on the floor with delight.

But how true it is! A background for books will do wonders. We don't expect children to be born liking Beethoven and Brahms. We take them to concerts, buy records, have them take music lessons. We don't expect them to be born understanding great art. We take them to galleries, have them study art, and are grateful if, after it all, they have a liking and some understanding of it. We even take children to museums and restored villages and antiquities so that they may appreciate old things of beauty and understand better what they came from.

But books! Often that is something else again. Money is spent for concerts and records. Part of their education, we say. Money is spent for pictures and trips to galleries. Education again. But a book! "Books are so expensive!" We buy space hats at $3.98, and real leather holsters with a brace of guns for the price of three or four books. The guns and the space hats are outgrown. But books are never outgrown. The ones the children love, whether they be classics or the Bobbsey Twins, give a lifelong satisfaction, teach a lesson, carry them "lands away," are treasured and handed on to their children. Books expensive? It is the space hat that is expensive.

When I think of children and books and of the opportunities we older folks miss to bring the two together I could weep. And when I see how important parents are to children, how wise the children think their parents are, how they adore them, the mean and cross parents included, I ache with the pain of the lost chances. Not only do we lose the chance to show the children what fun books are, but we are losing an opportunity to get close to our children, to have something wonderful in common. Childhood is so short. If we miss it, it is gone forever. We must do what we can quickly.

I suppose the first thing we can do is to have books at home. So many homes today have no room for books. And it is surprising how many lost library books turn up in the attic when mother cleans house. Why books in the attic? A child should have books around him from the minute he is able to sit up. And I mean it literally. A friend of mine did just that. She happened to love books herself, so Bunny had books from the beginning. I can well remember my astonishment at finding that baby sitting quietly looking at books from her bookshelf. And her mother told me that in the mornings they would find her in her crib with a book she had been able to reach from the bed. Having books in the house makes books seem as natural as breathing. To such a child, surrounded by books, when the time comes for him to read there is nothing strange about it.

Someone is sure to say, "Won't young children tear the books?" Yes, they do, quite frankly. But there is a difference in kinds of tearing. A child should never be allowed to wantonly tear a book, or anything else, for that matter. He can be trained not to. If a book is torn because little hands are awkward and cannot hold it so carefully, or worn from many lookings and reading, I would say that book should be replaced. To wait until a child is old enough to handle a treasure is waiting until the child is too old to receive the first impression of books. Recently I took four picture books to a three-year-old friend. With what joy he received them! He disappeared from sight. We found him on the sofa sitting up straight and good, looking at his books, laughing with joy . . . and they were bottom side up. Once I gave a two-year-old boy *The Big Book of Real Trucks.* As long as I was there Jimmy had not yet gotten past the end papers which were covered with all kinds of trucks. He wouldn't let a page be turned until he had taken it all in.

One of the first books to give a baby is *Johnny Crow's Garden.* I am always a little frightened to give it without first warning the parents that it is pure nonsense, not to expect any sense, and to please read it to the child, for he will like it. In Dicken's *The Magic Fishbone,* the Fairy Grandmarino stamps her foot when the King asks the reason for his taking the fishbone to the princess. "The reason for this and the reason for that!" she cried. "All you grownups want is reason. No reason! There!" For so many delightful things there seems to be no reason, and yet, a child loves the illogical, the unreasonable, the nonsense. Once I gave *Johnny Crow's Garden* to a friend for her baby. I was going through Washington Square one spring day. There sat Roddy and his mother on a bench. His mother, for my benefit, would recite:

"The lion
Had a green and yellow . . ."

"tie on," Roddy would finish.

"But the Bear
Had nothing . . ."

his mother went on, "to wear" finished Roddy. "Tie on" meant nothing to the baby but sounds, yet he loved it. After all, the whole meant nothing anyway. "No reason! There!" The pictures of a lion sitting very smugly on a park bench with a green tie on, and the bear being measured for a suit of clothes—"the ape took his measure with a tape"—entrances children.

At the top of the list, almost, of things to do to bring children and books together, is just plain ordinary friendliness in regard to books—talking about books at home, sharing favorite books, father telling what he read and the boy telling his favorites. Don't be critical. He has a right to his opinion. So many times the critic has not even read the book he criticizes, or forgets the charm of some book he read as a boy. The boy has read it. If you think his taste is bad, subtly try to change it by giving him interesting, better books. Don't argue. That will do no good. He has read it. He likes it. So what! It is so easy to spoil a book, to spoil reading, for a child by forcing something on him. Recently I heard a grandmother lamenting, "I don't understand why Peter [aged twelve] does not read the classics." What is a classic? Classics are being made all the time. The classics the grandmother was thinking of went back years. She was not up on the more recent classics. We know right now certain books that will be called classics tomorrow. How long does it take to make a classic, I wonder. Would thirty years do it? Then *The Story of Doctor Dolittle* is a classic. And some of the so-called classics, if re-examined, would not stand the test today, not even of the grandparents who had read them as children.

Enthusiasm is a great help in interesting children in books; a little advertising goes a long way, I find. A few enthusiastic remarks about a book get an instant response—that is, if the child has confidence in your taste. Alex's "It's the bloodiest and the best book I ever read," about *Michael Strogoff, Courier to the Czar,* made the book circulate through a whole seventh grade. They knew Alex liked books that were good. If you are trying to interest a child in a book, don't pick out that beautiful soulful passage. Pick out the exciting adventure, or whatever it is that you think would interest him. Put yourself in his place. A teacher I know reads aloud a great deal to her class. She knows her books well before she begins. If she cannot read the whole book she picks her passage carefully, and without fail, the majority of her class comes to the library for the book.

Give books as gifts. Let no birthday or Christmas go by without a few books; not books that *you* like, books that *he* will like, the boy. Maybe he is a practical soul who would love *The Boy Mechanic* book. The gift of that book might well be the one that would lead him to more books—not necessarily "classics," or even story books, but a love of books for what they can do for him. Let a child feel that he is doing the selecting. As someone said once in regard to this matter, "I wouldn't like to go to a restaurant and have an unordered meal shoved at me."

Let children buy books themselves once in a while. Let them pick them out. If their choice is bad they will learn, and it is not a very costly mistake. At one of our book fairs one mother was the bane of our existences. She had her two boys look over the books before she arrived to see what they would like to buy. When mother arrived the trouble began. There were tears, arguments, and sometimes no books. Once, I remember, her boy picked out *Homer Price.* He was the kind of boy who would have benefited by it. He needed the humor of Homer. Mother liked books on rocks. Result? They bought a book on rocks.

Children are very careful with money of their own. They will pore over books, not wanting to make a bad choice. As Christopher Morley said "There are some books definitely worth owning." They are not the same to any two people. What I would like to own is not what you would like. Children are the same way. *Kit and Kat,* that book I spoke of earlier, was a book John might well want to own—the first book he ever found easy to read. Clifton Fadiman, one of the world's great readers, said that no book ever meant so much to him as *The Overall Boys.* It was exciting to him, this story in the simplest words, because he could read it to himself.

Mary Lee returned *The Good Master*. It was the last day of school when all books had to be in. "Oh dear!" she said, as she put the book on the library desk, "I do wish I could finish it." I felt like a heel. There is nothing worse than not being able to finish a good story, and that was such a good one. "I am sorry," I said, "but I have to have all books back. Why don't you buy a copy?" I knew the family could well afford to buy books. Happily, at my suggestion, she rushed to telephone her mother if she might let me get her a copy of *The Good Master*. She came back crestfallen. "Mother said I can't." "Why?" I demanded, very annoyed with the mother. "She says I know it by heart. I've read it four times." Now *I* contend that that book was the very one Mary Lee should own. A book you want to read and read is the very one to put in your library. Caroline's mother said, "Caroline wants *Merry Lips* for Christmas. Why, I'll bet she's read it thirty-five times." The very book for Caroline to own.

We were having our annual Book Sale in the library. One of the older boys had ordered *Get Tough*: The Art of Self Defense, written by a captain in the Marines. Derry, who wasn't more than eight, saw the paper-backed book put aside. How he craved it! Each day after school he would come in to look at it. "Why don't you buy it?" I asked him. It was only a dollar. "My mother thinks I'm too tough already," he answered. One night, after his daily look at the book, he stopped just as he was going out of the door. "Say," he said over his shoulder, "I might ask my dad. He's a tough guy too." I have a feeling that it would have been a good "buy" for Derry. When a child wants a book *that* badly, no one knows what it might mean to him.

It is nice to build up a library of what are known as "classics," but better to build up a library first beginning with books the child knows and likes to reread and have fun with. Then can come the classics. Ones like *The Good*

Master may be classics of tomorrow. Who knows? It was the reading and rereading of *Heidi* that made it a classic.

Years ago, Dorothy Canfield Fisher was asked a series of questions about children's reading. Do children read too much? Should older children read adult books? Are good detective stories bad for children? Should children read about sex? She said, in answer:

> I find my vocal chords spasmodically tensing for a questioning bellow, "*Which* children?" or, rather, "Which child?" What's the answer to the questions: Are good detective stories bad for people? How should sex be treated in books for people? The only answer I can think of is, "I'll tell you that if you'll tell me how big is a house?" And when my interlocutor asks blankly, "What kind of a house?" answer him, "What kind of people?" Do children read too much? Some do and some don't. Isn't it the obvious job of every parent to know which kind his children are? How about detective stories? They might be just what's needed by a boy who's slow in mastering the mechanics of reading. Often the trouble with such a child is that his interest has not been held closely enough to push him through the difficulties of the printed word. If he is strong-nerved and robust, not timid, not unduly sensitive, detective stories might be the making of him intellectually because, through them, he might acquire that speed in reading which is essential if he's to get much use out of books. But because that is true, you wouldn't want your high-strung, impressionable, afraid-of-the-dark little girl of the same age to read them, would you? But they are both "children." And only a parent, teacher, aunt, or someone who knows them well, can tell the difference between them as to which are best for them. Furthermore, in the case of even one child, what's best for him now may be stale, old fodder six months from now. A growing girl, who now would be bored or repelled or bewildered by even a wise, humane treatment of sex problems in a book, might, before she is an inch taller, be needing just that and nothing else. Only by daily, comfortable, intimate, frank talk on all sorts of topics can one keep any track of a child's book needs. To supply them blindly, out of book lists, even good book lists without which nobody can make

a home, is exactly on a par with the old-woman habit of trying out every remedy for rheumatism which has benefited a neighbor's maladies, whether they were rheumatic or not.

What are parents, for, anyway?*

A child's interest is a good starting point for a love of books. Donald's interest in boats started him on sea stories, and led to an interest in many kinds of stories. Andrea's love of horse stories led from just pure horse story to stories with riding in them, and finally to books of all kinds. It doesn't always happen that a child who loves facts will be led into loving fiction, but sometimes it does.

We know that children read for three reasons: To learn to read (either the beginning reader or the child having trouble learning to read, and there's a difference); for information ("It tells me what I want to know."); for fun (and this doesn't necessarily mean just reading fiction, as many adults seem to think it should).

Children who are learning to read have to have books to begin on, like Clifton Fadiman's *The Overall Boys.* Fortunate we are that we have many easy-to-read interesting books for those children. The older children who are having trouble need books easy to read but with stories or facts that interest them. Many a child has learned to read by reading about radio or snakes or cats, or some other thing that he had an interest in. It is not as easy to find books for these children. Simple stories are likely to be too babyish in story and illustration.

All children need to read for information. Whether it be as simple as a grocery list or an article in an encyclopedia, he will need to be able to read it—and comprehend it, what's more. It is too much to expect a young child, or even a slightly older one, to read a long article and pick out the important facts. The average college student is not too good at note-taking or fact-finding. The mechanics of reading is so difficult for the little child, it is with effort that he reads

* *Saturday Review of Literature,* November 16, 1929.

through a long paragraph of an encyclopedia. He doesn't know how to skim yet, and pick the statement that means a great deal. Today we have many wonderful fact books on all subjects that are fairly easy reading, and the authors of these books seem to know just the facts the children want.

Reading for fun is something most of us want for children, even those of us who do not enjoy reading ourselves. But we have to remember that fun means something different to each of us. If John likes to read about electricity better than "Ali Baba and the Forty Thieves," that is *his* fun. Not only have we the old folks' tendency to expect children to read only fiction for fun, but we also expect each and every one of them to like what we think they ought to like. An adult would think he was stupid if he liked everything his neighbors liked. Yet, that is what many of us expect of children. All children should like *Black Beauty* . . . if *we* happen to have liked it. All children should read *Mary Poppins.* All should like *Alice in Wonderland.*

Children do read the old books, the classics. They read a great deal of serious reading. They also like other things, lighter things, as we do. First they must know how to read easily enough for it to be a real pleasure. It is like learning how to shift gears on a car. At first we have to think every time we do it. Then it becomes automatic so we can enjoy the scenery as we drive. It is the same way with children and reading. At first they have to think of every word. Then, finally, they can really enjoy the "scenery" as they go along. To read aloud is for them (and for many of us old ones, too) a double duty. First they have to know a word, then they have to pronounce it, hesitate if there is a comma, drop their voices if there is a period, and if they can manage all that, they still have to know what it all means. Many children can read great big things without knowing anything about which they are reading. What *is* reading? Is it just to be able to read words, or is it to know and enjoy what we are reading?

Some people are so eager to have their children read the right things they give them certain books too soon. When a mother bragged that her boy in the fourth grade was reading *Westward Ho* I felt badly. He wouldn't get from it what had made it live so long. And perhaps he would be bored by it and never try again when he was old enough to understand. Too, a precocious child often starts beyond the "baby" books. His parents read him things meant for older children. True, he will enjoy listening to big words and can "take" quite advanced stories, but then, he cannot go back to *Millions of Cats, Peter Rabbit,* and others he should not grow up without. You may say, "What hurt if he miss them?" A great deal of hurt. The world knows them. They are part of his heritage of literature. They are, as said before, a common language. To miss a whole section out of one's literary life is too bad.

What about books you do not want your child to read? It is a wonderful thing about children and books—and life, for that matter. They see in things only what they have experienced. Once a youngster brought me a dollar she had earned collecting inch worms. She wanted me to buy her a copy of *The Three Musketeers.* She was a bright twelve-year-old, well able to read the book, and a particularly refreshing child. I bought the book, had it home over the week end, and for the first time in years had a chance to reread it. I was horrified! The musketeers climbed in ladies' windows, and not just for exercise, I am sure. When I had read it before when I was young, it had meant nothing to me. What I thought then, I don't remember. Now it made me realize that our fear that children will get things from books that we don't want them to get is pretty groundless. They see what they know. The rest is not even meditated on. The average parent has *entente* enough with her child, I think, to say "You are not ready for this yet," and the child will agree. Some parents believe in letting children read anything they wish. As Mrs. Fisher said, "Which child?"

To sum it all up, if you want children to read, *give them books*. Buy books, borrow from the library, surround them with books and read them books, and listen to them talk about books, and talk to them about books. Make books such a part of their lives that they will think of reading like breathing—that is, just accept it as naturally as being alive.

V

"Not a word o' readin' in it."

PICTURE BOOKS

THE VERY LITTLE BOY looked over the librarian's stock. It was his first trip to the library by himself. Finally, his face shining, he came up to her desk. "This is an awful nice book," he said, "just an *awful* nice book. It's all pictures, not a word o' readin' in it."

Picture books are "awful nice," with their lovely illustrations, beautiful format, and amusing stories. A good picture book must have those things. There must be pictures that appeal to a child, clear, bright, beautiful, humorous, with details of the little things they know. The pictures must tell the story, for the little child, when the book has been read to him many times, loves to "read" them back to himself. "I *read* the *pictures,*" said the small boy. The story must not be too long. Too much text does not belong in a picture book. The story must have a real point or plot, simple, sometimes just one little point to be made, something to be worked toward and achieved.

The words should be lovely, good to read aloud, meaningful, for children remember words and often use them themselves afterwards. The text in picture books is not usually easy to read. They are not really the books for beginning readers. They are the books, though, *that make the reader begin,* that give him his first love of books and the desire to read to himself.

How the children live in their books! I was talking with a grandmother and naturally we discussed children's books. "Do your grandchildren know *Mike Mulligan and His Steam Shovel*?" I asked. "Do they know *Mike Mulligan*!" she replied. "They were being driven along a road one day when suddenly they shrieked, 'There's Mary Ann!' The chauffeur put on the brakes hard, thinking it was a playmate. But it was a steam shovel."

Little Toot, the little tugboat, is a real personality to children. David, at four, announced, "I made a poem."

Little Toot, Little Toot,
Went to town
To buy some fresh smoke
to wear.

When I repeated it to someone and said "new smoke," he quietly corrected me: "No, *fresh* smoke."

Curious George, the hilarious monkey book, was so much loved by one four-year-old that he wanted to name his baby brother Curious George.

Good picture books go the year round, regardless of their own particular season. *Paddy's Christmas* is one of these. "What's Christmas?" asked Paddy, the bear cub. "It's pretty, it's lots of fun, and it makes you feel good from the inside out. Whatever it is, I want one." He finally found out. It was doing things for others, that was it. Children love the story with its sweet pictures, in browns and yellows, of the bears asleep in the cave, and little Paddy waking them up. How the children laugh when Paddy wakes them up all over again! Children love to "play" it, too. Once a group of kindergarten children were going to "play" it. One little boy just didn't want to be anything. His teacher, a peppy gal, said, "Wouldn't you like to be Uncle Bear?" "Nope." "Wouldn't you just *love* to be Paddy?" "Nope. Wanta be a bush." So he was the bush that Paddy hid behind.

A little boy was starting toward the library desk with a book about planes. Suddenly he stopped and said to himself,

"Guess I'd better take a book about jets." They know so much these days about mechanical things.

While boys are wanting cars and planes and books about wrecking machines, from the minute they begin to look, the little girls are wanting pictures of babies and soft animals, and family stories. *April's Kittens,* with its soft black kitties, and *Billy and Blaze,* about a little boy and his horse, are favorites with little girls. Instead of *The Big Book of Real Trucks* they are looking at *The A B C Bunny* and *Fancy Be Good,* the story of a naughty little kitten.

Although each child is different from every other one, there is a book for every child. They look at books purely for fun but that fun is multiplied many times when it can be shared with mother, father, or big brother. We can't force children to like any particular books but our enthusiasm will help "sell" it to a child. Subtly we can say, "This is a wonderful book. My, I remember how I loved that part about the tiger [or whatever]." Pick out something that will interest that particular child.

Some children are ready for certain books before other children are. It depends a lot on the background and what reading and looking have been done earlier. Children who have been read to and shown pictures from the earliest moment are ready sooner to sit quietly and listen.

It is better and less confusing to the child to have a few books at a time. Good picture books will be looked at again and again. Then once in a while a new one may be introduced. When first a child listens to a story he may be just liking the sound of the words, but he soon becomes accustomed to sitting still and listening. Children have a real interest in new words. A three-year-old ahead of me in church a few Sundays ago picked up words the minister used. "Frontier," she whispered to her mother. Then "Frontier again."

Four-year-old Johnny sat on the steps as his father came out of their house. "Daddy, I'm discouraged," he said. "Why

Johnny, what's the trouble?" his father asked anxiously. "Daddy, what's discouraged?" said Johnny.

An editor friend had a manuscript for a picture book she wished tried with a child. One of her associates took it home to read to his five-year-old. The next morning he reported: "When I came to the word *jail* I wondered if he'd know what it was, so I said, 'Do you know what that means?' 'Isn't it a little like a penitentiary?' " the five-year-old asked.

There are games that can be played about books that help pass the time when riding in the car, or just for fun at the dinner table—games that even the little ones can take part in. Starting nursery rhymes and letting someone finish them; guessing answers to questions about books such as "Who found the house where seven dwarfs lived?" "Whose father was put in a pie by Mrs. McGregor?" "What did Mary Ann do . . . go to the movies? Read a book? Dig a cellar?" "Who gave his clothes to three tigers?" And so on.

Very little children like to "play" stories. Carol, at three, played *Little Black Sambo,* taking most of the parts herself. Her mother, working in the kitchen, would be one tiger with an umbrella hooked in her apron. Carol also played *The Three Little Pigs,* playing all the parts. Her house was a blanket over a chair. She was inside for the pigs and outside as the wolf, "huffing and puffing to blow the house down."

Below are some of the well known editions of the picture books children love best. There are hundreds of other good books. These will suggest the kinds children have loved and treasured through the years.

Favorite Picture Books

Johnny Crow's Garden. Written and illustrated by Leslie Brooke. Warne. Nonsense rhymes and amusing pictures. It seems that when the author was a small boy he and his brother played a game with their father; father would say a sentence and the boys would make one to rhyme with it.

Later, Leslie Brooke, who had become an artist, made a book of these rhymes. Ages 1-5.

The Real Mother Goose. With pictures by Blanche Fisher. Rand. Over 300 rhymes and 170 bright-colored pictures. A very popular Mother Goose with children.

Tall Mother Goose. Pictured by Feodor Rojankovsky. Harper. A hundred familiar rhymes with 150 pictures. Very gay and humorous, a tall narrow book. Children adore the pictures. His animals are particularly wonderful. You can buy the pictures in a portfolio for framing for the nursery wall.

Book of Nursery and Mother Goose Rhymes. Doubleday. Illustrated by the typical Marguerite De Angeli illustrations in beautiful soft colors. It is such a big book, so beautiful, it seems just the thing for grandmother to have on hand when the grandchildren come to visit.

Lavender's Blue, compiled in England by Kathleen Lines and illustrated by Harold Jones. Watts. Includes all the old favorites, and many lesser known; counting rhymes and riddles. It is illustrated in full color, dainty and beautiful. Another to use *with* the child rather than for him to use by himself.

Ring O' Roses. Illustrated by Leslie Brooke. Warne. A classic Mother Goose. Less complete but a joy because of the pictures.

A B C Book. C. B. Falls. Doubleday. The alphabet was cut in wood blocks and printed in bright colors. No text. Each letter is an animal chosen from zoo and farmyard. Ages 2-4.

A B C Bunny. Written and illustrated by Wanda Gag. Coward. The little rabbit's adventures told in picture and verse. Every letter is an adventure of Bunny's and he scampers through the pages from A to Z. The book is large and flat with soft black-and-white pictures. A book that will be loved and treasured. Ages 2-5.

A is for Annabelle. Written and illustrated by Tasha Tudor. Oxford. An alphabet book in verse, with charming daintily colored pictures in which two little girls play with Annabelle, an old-fashioned doll. It delights little girls. Ages 3-5.

A for the Ark. Written and illustrated by Roger Duvoisin. Lothrop. God commanded Noah to take two from every kind of animal so he went straight through the alphabet. Ages 4-6.

A B C. Written and illustrated by Charlotte Steiner. Hanover House. A charming alphabet book of children today, doing things all children do. Bright-colored pictures. Text rhymes. Ages 3-6.

Big Book of Real Trucks. Text and pictures by George Zaffo. Grosset. Big, realistic illustrations in color of the different kinds of trucks. There are many books in this series that interest little boys.

Little Auto, Little Train, Little Sail Boat, Little Farm, Little Fire Engine, Cowboy Small, to mention only a few written and illustrated by Lois Lenski. Oxford. Mr. Small, looking like the eternal small boy, goes through the simplest adventures, having to do with driving a car, saddling a horse, sailing, working on the farm. Children learn a great deal, too, since the information is simple and authentic. Children of three years old love to look at them and listen to the stories. At six they love to read them to themselves. David who had just begun to read made his first trip to the library to select books for himself. He came nine times that first day, each time taking a different book about "Mr. Small." When his teacher asked him if he were not bothering the librarian, coming so much, he replied, "Oh no. She is simply delighted. You ought to see her face." Ages 1-8.

Blueberries for Sal. Written and illustrated by Robert McCloskey. Viking. A delightful picture book about Maine. It has a simple and adequate plot, and charming and amusing pictures. Sal and her mother go blueberrying. A baby bear goes blueberrying with his mother. The two babies, in lingering to eat berries, get lost, and each is following the wrong mother. Eventually, after not too much trouble, each finds his own. It is as simple as that but very satisfying to a three- or four-year-old child. And to the parent who is reading it, as well. Ages 2-5.

The Tale of Peter Rabbit. Written and illustrated by Beatrix Potter. Warne. Every child should have his own "Peter Rabbit" books in the *original* edition. The tiny books with the adorable illustrations of the English countryside are very much loved by children. The story of Peter is never old. An old lady in a book shop complained, "But these are all *old* books you are showing me." "Yes, madam," the bookseller replied, "but the children are always new." There is a first time for every child. Don't forget that. Other books by Beatrix Potter are equally charming. Ages 2-7.

Angus and the Ducks. Written and illustrated by Marjorie Flack. Doubleday. The amusing adventures of a Scottie puppy whose curiosity led him to crawl under the hedge and he was chased by the ducks. There is very little text and very delightful illustrations in color. Loved by very young children. Ages 2-5. *Wait for William, Walter the Lazy Mouse* are some other books by the same author.

Little Toot. Written and illustrated by Hardie Gramatky. Putnam. A "new" classic for children, for we are sure it will be one, is the perfect example of an author's getting right down inside an inanimate object so you feel its reality. The pictures of this little Tug Boat who didn't want to take any responsibility, just play, until a storm came up and he was needed, are bright and amusing. It is the kind of a book that, when you have finished the last page, the child says, "No, read it again." The interesting thing is, the reader does not tire of it either. Ages 2-8.

A Child's Good Night Book. Margaret Wise Brown. Illustrated by Jean Charlot. Scott. This is called "the sleepy book" by children who love it. Her words are few but beautiful. Everything goes to sleep. A perfect bedtime book. Ages 2-5.

Goodnight Moon. Margaret Wise Brown. Harper. A companion to the other one, shows, from page to page, a gradually darkening room, as a bunny in a big bed dozes off. Good night everything. Ages 2-5.

The Story of Babar, the Elephant. Written and illustrated by Jean de Brunhoff. Random House. Babar charms children. They love the story of the little elephant who ran away from the jungle and went to live in the city with an understanding old lady. The pictures are as amusing as the story.

The Growing Story. Ruth Krauss. Illustrated by Phyllis Rowland. Harper. A small boy watches the grass, flowers, chickens grow but does not seem to realize that he, too, is growing until he puts on last year's clothes. So simply told, yet so full of meaning to a child. Ages 3-7.

The Story of Little Black Sambo. Written and illustrated by Helen Bannerman. Lippincott. This is one of the most popular books ever for little children and don't let anyone tell you it isn't. First published in 1900, this book is a real classic. As you likely know, it is a very funny story of a little Indian boy, the beautiful new clothes his mother bought him, and his adventures with three tigers. Children want to read it again and again and again. Be sure to get the *original* edition. It is much more fun. Ages 2-8.

Mike Mulligan and His Steam Shovel. Written and illustrated by Virginia Lee Burton. Houghton. An absolute "must" for little boys, and when you read it aloud you will see why. Mike Mulligan takes his old-fashioned steam shovel to dig a cellar for a town hall. The steam shovel operator is so interested in working, particularly because a little boy is watching him, that he forgets to leave a way to get out. Lots of fun. Others by the same author: *The Little House, Katy and the Big Snow, Choo Choo.* Ages 2-8.

Mike's House. Julia Sauer. Illustrated by Don Freeman. Viking. A little boy knows the public library as "Mike's House" because that is where he gets *Mike Mulligan and His Steam Shovel.* How the little boy gets lost and finally finds the library is a cute story which children who know *Mike Mulligan* love. Ages 5-8.

The Story About Ping. Marjorie Flack. Illustrated by Kurt Wiese. Viking. A little Chinese duck lived on a houseboat. Every night he was slow in getting on the boat and got spanked. A librarian going through the Children's Room saw a big brother reading *Ping* to his little brother. As she went past she heard the little fellow say, "Hurry up, stupid, or he'll get spanked again." It is one of the nicest stories for children. A lovely book to own, with its lovely bright pictures. Ages 2-7.

Millions of Cats. Written and illustrated by Wanda Gag. Coward. When this book came out it made quite a furor. It is told in the folk-tale manner with plenty of repetition, and a perfect story, one that children learn almost by heart. The old man went out to find a kitty for his wife and was suddenly confronted by "hundreds of cats, thousands of cats, millions and billions and trillions of cats." What he did and how it all turned out is perfect. The black-and-white illustrations are quaint and lovely. Ages 2-7.

Make Way for Ducklings. Written and illustrated by Robert McCloskey. Viking. A gay story with delightful pictures about Mr. and Mrs. Mallard and their family of eight ducklings who live on an island in the Charles River, and think nothing of marching across a Boston street and holding up the traffic. Suggested by a true incident. It is a large and beautiful book and won the Caldecott Medal for the nicest picture book of the year. Ages 2-7.

If I Ran the Zoo. Written and illustrated by Dr. Seuss (Theodore Geisel). Random House. Gerald McGrew thought up a new kind of zoo. He let all the animals out of the old one and began collecting the most astounding "camp meeting" of animals you ever saw. The children just adore this book, and all the others by the same author. Nonsense at its funniest, with funny pictures. Other books: *And to Think That I Saw it on Mulberry Street, McElligott's Pool,*

Scrambled Eggs Super, Thidwick, The Bighearted Moose, Horton Hatches an Egg, On Beyond Zebra. Take a Dr. Seuss book when you are going on a long trip by car or train. Your youngster will be quiet for hours. More interesting to children than the comics. How's that? Ages 3-10.

Marshmallow. Written and illustrated by Clare Newberry. Harper. Marshmallow was a baby bunny and the story of his friendship with Oliver, a cat, is full of beauty and humor and understanding of children and animals. The soft black-and-white pictures make you want to touch them. You can almost feel the cat's fur. Others by the same author: *April's Kittens, Smudge, Mittens.* Ages 5-9.

Rabbit's Revenge. Written and illustrated by Kurt Wiese. Coward. A daring group of rabbits gave Old Man Shivers his comeuppance because he schemed to make himself a suit of rabbit's fur. Done with very funny pictures and brief text. Ages 5-8. As one very young reviewer wrote, "This book shows that you can always win if you work together."

The Park Book. Charlotte Zolotow. Pictures by H. A. Rey. Harper. Simple text and gay pictures in color tell of the events in a park from early morning until dark. It pleases little children very much. Ages 4-6.

White Snow, Bright Snow. Alvin Tresselt. Illustrated by Roger Duvoisin. Lothrop. Conveys the softness and beauty of snowfall both in words and pictures. Not much story but very satisfying to little children, very beautiful to read. Other books by Tresselt that are similar in quality and looks: *Follow the Wind, Hi, Mister Robbin, I Saw the Sea Come In.* Ages 3-6.

Boats on the River. Marjorie Flack. Illustrations by Jay Hyde Barnum. Doubleday. All kinds of boats in a big bright picture book that boys, especially, love to look at. About a busy river flowing through a great city with all the different kinds of boats on it. Full of action and pleases children of different ages. Ages 5-8.

Down, Down the Mountain. Written and illustrated by

Ellis Creadle. Nelson. How Hetty and Hank who lived high up in the Blue Ridge Mountains raised some fine turnips which they hoped to trade for some squeaky creaky shoes, and how their kindness almost made them lose. A delightful story. Ages 6-8.

The Biggest Bear. Written and illustrated by Lynd Ward. Houghton. Johnny decided to shoot a bear so he could have a skin on his barn door like other people. He brought home a cub which was too big. He tried to get rid of it in the woods but it kept coming back. Finally he found another solution. The large brown pictures are as interesting as the story. Caldecott Medal. Ages 6-9.

Beady Bear. Written and illustrated by Don Freeman. Viking. Beady Bear left a note, "I have gone to live where bears live." He went to the cave, as all bears should. Little children will love this as a bedtime story. Ages 3-6.

Georgie. Written and illustrated by Robert Bright. Doubleday. Georgie, a very friendly little ghost, lived in the Whittakers' attic and haunted their home until Mr. Whittaker took the creak out of the stair and the rattle out of the windows. He found another place but he was very lonesome. Eventually the creek and rattle came back, and so did Georgie. You'll love and laugh at Georgie. A *first* ghost and Hallowe'en story for children. Ages 5-8.

Little Tim and the Brave Sea Captain. Written and illustrated by Edward Ardizzone. Oxford. A beautiful picture book in which the illustrations look like wash drawings. Tim, a five-year-old hero, went out to visit a ship with his friend the Captain. He stowed away and was put to work. There was a storm and Tim proved himself a hero. Another book by same author: *Tim to the Rescue.*

Peter Churchmouse. Written and illustrated by Margot Austin. Dutton. A hungry church mouse and a cat who was supposed to clear the church of rats (not Peter), and had an adventure trying to get cheese for Peter. Children love this story. Ages 4-7.

Noël for Jeanne Marie. Françoise Seignobose. Scribner. Jean Marie and her pet sheep celebrated Christmas together. An absolutely charming story with equally charming pictures. Others by the same author: *Small Trot, Briquette.*

Journey Cake, Ho! Ruth Sawyer. Illustrated by Robert McCloskey. Viking. A new version of a favorite folk tale. A duck, a pig, a cow, a donkey and Johnny, all chase the Journey cake. Wonderful pictures full of action. Ages 4-8.

VI

"Not too fairy."

FOLK AND FAIRY TALES

"The truce of the wolf," wrote the girl in her book report, "is a perfect book for people who like fairy tales that aren't too fairy." As a matter of fact, most fairy stories are not very "fairy."

Once in a while we find people who say they do not like fairy tales. I think they do not know what fairy tales are. The word fairy does not mean what we usually think it does. It comes from an Old French word meaning "enchantment," to be carried away to another world where strange things may happen. It is true that in many fairy tales queer little people who perform magic often appear; sometimes they are funny and sometimes horrible, sometimes like what we have come to think fairies are—dainty little creatures. But there do not have to be "fairies" in a "fairy tale." For the most part, when we use the word "fairy tales" we are referring to folk tales, or those stories handed down by word of mouth from the "folk" or people of a country. They were told wherever there were groups of people in those early days when they did not have lamps to read by and, probably, most people could not read. These tales, repeated from one person to another, one generation to the next—changed a bit in the retelling—had a very great importance, not only to them but to us today. They were told by homesick people in strange lands in their own language, and they kept the language alive for them. They were told to amuse and pass the time. Someone has said that storytelling died out in Ireland with the invention of the oil lamp and modern manufacturing methods, for storytelling by the light of a candle was quite different. And when people got together in "bees" to make things, the storyteller would come to entertain them.

From these old folk tales we learn a great deal about the people. We know their superstitions and beliefs, their fears and loves, their ways of living and the environment in which they lived. In Russia where the cold is feared, their folk tales bring in that fear and often the cold and snow are personified. In India, the tigers and elephants, jackals, and famine are part of their lives and are in their stories. The food they ate (delicious khichri, made of rice and butter with spices) ; their trees, (the banyan tree), all appear in the background. Trolls and giants are in the North; Difs and Topsches in Albania; the wee red man in Ireland; pixes and brownies in the British Isles—just to mention a few.

Throughout all of the folk tales of all the countries we find many similar stories we call variants. The plot will be similar, or a device similar. From the very earliest times there have been Cinderella stories, so called because the device of the shoe was used. Even the very Irish "Billy Beg and His Bull" used the shoe. No one knows why similar stories cropped up all over the world from India to Europe to America. Someone had the theory that at a certain stage of civilization people had the same beliefs and superstitions. Others think the stories were carried by travelers and traders. Indian stories are about the oldest of all, several thousand years old. They were written down only about seventy-five years ago. The collector, in one instance, who was the wife of a British official, talked with the people as they waited to put their cases before her husband. From them she got bits of stories.

Even in that-not-so-long-ago, the villages of India had storytellers, and on hot nights, before the breeze came up, the people would bring their mats to the village street where the storyteller entertained them until it was cool enough to sleep.

The *Arabian Nights* go back no one knows how far, but they were written down by a Frenchman in the eighteenth century. At first, people thought he made them up. They also thought that the tales all came from Persia. We know now that they are from the whole Eastern world: China, India, Arabia, Persia. Do you remember the fascinating story about Scheherezade? (spelled in many different ways). She was the daughter of the Grand Vizier and a very clever girl. She was learned in the history and poetry and legends of her country. Her father had the unpleasant duty of finding wives for the Sultan, unpleasant because the Sultan, hating women, had each wife killed the day after he married her. When Scheherezade offered herself, thinking she could save the women of Persia from their fate, she made an arrangement with her sister. The sister begged the Sultan to let her spend the night in the room with them, since it would be her sister's last night on earth. During the night, she asked Scheherezade for a story. Scheherezade began a story but it was not finished when dawn came, so the Sultan let her live another day to finish it. The next night she started another story which remained unfinished, and so on it went, for a thousand and one nights. By that time the Sultan had fallen in love with her and would not have had her killed for anything.

Scheherezade is called "the greatest literary invention," for by use of this storyteller the tales of many nations are woven into a whole. Many of these stories are not suitable for children, and some of the ones that are in collections for children may not have been with the original. At any rate, children love them. They have the color and gorgeousness of the East. As someone said, "They are like light streaming through a stained-glass window." "Ali Baba and the Forty Thieves" and "Aladdin and His Wonderful Lamp" are the most popular with young people. In a sense, these tales are not genuine folklore, and they were not handed down in quite the same way, nor perhaps made up by the "folk." Some people think they go back to Charlemagne's court.

Real folk tales have similarities in form as well as in plot. There is a rule of three, if you have noticed, in the old tales—for instance, three brothers, the oldest two "as clever fellows as ever ate peas with a fork," while the youngest one "hardly knew enough to blow on his potatoes when they were hot"; but he usually comes out ahead, to our delight. Three little pigs, three bears. The hero performs three deeds. If he travels he goes for "three days and three nights without stopping." The plots are straightforward, concise, with no complications. I like them, I think, because they are so clear-cut. The good person is good and the evil person is evil. The evil one gets his comeuppance, and the hero, although he may be boiled in oil, comes out handsomer that he was before. How children rejoice when the cross old woman tumbles down the stairs! "And that was the end of the old woman." How they rejoice when the old witch is killed in her own oven, or the dragon is slain, or the troll killed by the biggest Billy Goat Gruff! Mrs. Becker, in her book *The First Adventures in Reading,* says, "Don't worry overmuch about the horrid results of Grimm. Watch a child read the funnies. See if he shivers at the sight of some one who dropped from a height and landed on his head. They have previously disconnected the idea that it hurt. The same is true of folklore. Of course, there are some impressionable children who should be guarded against them. Parents would know." Whether or not a story is horrible depends a lot on the way it is read to children. In reading "Billy Beg and His Bull," when the Queen, Billy's mother, dies, it would be possible to read it in such a way that the children would be upset, just by the tone of voice. But if it is read "The Queen died and was buried and the King got a new Queen" without making any particular point of it, children are a lot more upset over the bull's death than over the Queen's.

I had a manuscript to read to the children. It was the story of a rooster who was eventually killed for Sunday dinner. When I finished the story there was a silence. Finally, one youngster said, "It was sad." Another said, "Couldn't they have had the rooster *almost* killed, and then saved at the end?" Then I read them what the editor said: "Fairy tales are cruel." With one voice, the children said, "But fairy tales always turn out all right." The children know with certainty that the hero will come out on top and the wicked king, or whoever, will get his just due.

Fairy tales, or folk tales, have vitality, personality, humor, both subtle and earthy. Most of them are written in beautiful language and imagery, quaint colloquial idioms. And as the little boy said, "I like fairy tales because they teach me to be kind." The girl who was kind to the choked stream and cleared away its leaves was rewarded. The little half-chick who wasn't kind to the fire, the brook, and the wind, suffered at their hands later on.

Each country has stamped its personality on its tales. The Finnish stories (one of the largest collections of folklore called *Kalevala*) are lusty. They love to laugh at their own characteristics, their stubbornness. They have matches with the devil—and win, of course. Their "Mighty Mikko" is a variant of "Puss in Boots" but the little fox is the hero instead of a cat, and it is a peasant story instead of a court story. Their humor is fun. Their story of the simple people back in the interior, "The Wise Men of Homola," is as modern as can be, and yet it is hundreds of years old. Human nature doesn't change.

The French stories are more sophisticated. Their "Cinderella" is one of the loveliest. From them we get "Red Riding Hood," "The White Cat"—yes, and "Bluebeard."

The Norse stories are especially interesting to children.

"The Three Billy Goats Gruff," "East of the Sun and West of the Moon," "Dapplegrim," "Princess on a Glass Hill"—one could go on for a long time naming favorites of the children.

The German, of course, we know through the Grimm Brothers, those funny little professors who collected their tales from the housewives, the shepherds, the common people; rightly were they called *Household Tales.* The brothers were anthropologists, interested in the beliefs of the people. It just happened that the children took them up in a big way—as they have other folk tales—for their adventure, magic and vitality. "Hänsel and Gretel," "Six Servants," "Rumplestiltskin," and others, are from Grimm.

The Russians, for all their trying to get rid of them, have some of the most beautiful folk tales in the world. They are, except for some little stories, more difficult, and more interesting to older children. "The Little Humpbacked Horse," "The Stolen Turnips," "Baba Yaga," "To Your Good Health," and the stories by Valery Carrick, to mention a few, are of interest to younger children. Arthur Ransome told, during the First World War when he was a correspondent in Russia, of the Russian soldiers stopping for tea along the roadside march, and as they rested they told old folk tales.

The Irish folk tales have charm quite their own, somehow untouched by those around them. Their quaint and humorous twist of speech, their love of the "little people" whom they respect, their beauty, make them among the most popular of stories with children. Until recently, their professional story-tellers (*shanache*) went about telling stories for "bed and breakfast."

The English stories show the influence of the Norse. They are quaint and folksy and are some of our most familiar tales.

All the countries of the world, I suspect, have folk literature. We have recently found tales from Africa and other far-off and primitive countries. Some of them are variants, and one wonders how they got them.

America has its own folklore, too. The American Indians had very beautiful stories, in which animals were characters. We have also the tall tales of Paul Bunyan, Pecos Bill, and others.

Each country has its own touches of originality. Those from Albania often began "On a year and a day . . ." Those from Spain, "Once there was and was not. . . ." Each country has its own little repetitions, rhymes and devices.

If you don't "hold with" magic—seven-league boots, water of life, trees that talk, and such—just remember that early peoples did not know scientific facts. If the hero had to get some place in a hurry to save the princess locked up by her wicked father in the tower three hundred miles away, how else could he get her out but with seven-league boots? No airplanes in those days. No telephones. No guns. In one step he was a hundred miles, in another step he was two hundred miles, and with the third step he was there . . . in time to save the princess. The early people explained things they didn't understand with magic. If the cream soured, the "little people" must be angry, so they were propitiated with a bowl of porridge left on the steps. Each country had its own strange creatures, its own kind of magic. The Finnish people sang things into being with magic runes.

These stories were not children's stories. They were told to grownups, with children probably listening in. But the children liked them and took them for themselves.

Fairy tales can do a great deal for children. They increase their imagination. If we all had more imagination about our fellow man there would be less trouble, fewer hurts, less cruelty. They cultivate our sense of humor. "The Jackal and the Alligator" and Howard Pyle's stories, to mention a few, are good for the serious child. They have an earthy kind of fun that calls forth a hearty laugh.

Without making any particular point of it, fairy tales do teach a lesson. The greedy one, the cruel one, the lazy one, are always in the wrong.

Fairy tales take us all around the world, showing us how other people live and think, what their humor is like, what they love and fear.

Fairy tales are escape from the hustle and bustle of today's world.

"Fairy tales are invaluable as a preparation for an appreciation of literature in later life. How can a child appreciate the magic of great poets if he has not been familiar with the mysterious forests, the high enchanted hills, the solitary castles, and the talking animals and birds of the fairy stories? Folklore is the first real literature that can be given to little children. It should not be denied them, for it serves as a gateway to all great literature, past and present," wrote Anne Eaton.*

"I like emagination because it is not real. We all know real things but not emaginary," wrote a small girl. These books and stories listed below are some of the favorite "emaginary" stories. There are many collections of folk tales. Many of them are for the story teller, many are for the students of folklore. I am telling you of those especially for children.

I suppose the first stories told to children, the very little children, are "The Three Billy Goats Gruff," "The Three Little Pigs," and "The Three Bears." Most parents know these themselves and probably tell them instead of reading them. There are some collections of stories that contain these very "young" and, at the same time, very old stories, with many others of interest to the youngest child.

Favorite Folk, Fairy, and Religious Tales

Told Under the Green Umbrella. Association for Childhood Education International. Macmillan. A collection of such stories. It contains such favorites as: "The Pancake," "The Old Woman and Her Pig," "The Three Billy Goats Gruff," "Travels of a Fox," "The Elves and the Shoemaker,"

* Eaton, Anne Thaxter, *Reading with Children,* Viking, p. 71.

"The Fisherman and His Wife," "Cinderella," "The Princess on a Glass Hill," and others. Good versions of the stories have been used throughout. It is a wonderful collection to own. Ages 5-8.

English Fairy Tales. Edited by Joseph Jacobs. Putnam. One of the earliest collections of the familiar English stories such as "Jack the Giant Killer," "Jack and the Bean Stalk," "Molly Whuppie," "Tom Tit Tot," "Whittington and His Cat." Jacobs has been called "The English Grimm." He wrote the stories in the colloquial speech as if an old nurse were telling them. These are stories every child should grow up with.

East o' the Sun and West o' the Moon. There are many good editions of these stories, some more complete than others. Ingri and Edgar d'Aulaire selected and illustrated a very beautiful edition. Peter C. Asbjornsen's and Jorgen Moe's is the classic edition. Macmillan. Gudrun Thorne-Thomsen retold some of the stories in a simple dramatic style. Row. Sigrid Undset made a fine collection called *True and Untrue.* Knopf. It is based on the Asbjornsen-Moe collection. It contains some stories not found in the other editions. The stories in these collections are childhood favorites, as: "Why the Sea is Salt," "Dapplegrim," "Gutbrand on the Hillside," "Buttercup," "East o' the Sun and West o' the Moon," "Seven Foals," "The Husband Who was to Mind the House."

Some of the East Indian tales are loved by little children, and are the first I tell in a story hour: "The Cat and the Parrot," available so far as I know, only in Sara Cone Bryant's *How to Tell Stories to Children,* a little book with suggestions for story-telling and a few stories as examples. It also includes the very popular story, "The Jackal and the Alligator" (found also in my own collection, *Fools and Funny Fellows*). Usually before I tell a story I make sure the children know what a jackal is. I don't ask if they know an alligator, for most children do. Then one day I had told the story to little children. They laughed and seemed to appreciate it. Something, I don't know what, made me ask at the end, "You do know what an alligator is?" One little boy making a motion with his hand, said, "One of those things you ride up and down on." Ever since I have asked if they knew what an alligator is too.

The Shoemaker's Apron, and *Mighty Mikko* and *Czechoslovakian Fairy Tales.* Parker Fillmore. Harcourt. Some wonderful and funny stories that children not only love to hear but love to dramatize, and later, love to read to themselves. "Budulinek," a special favorite with little children, "Forest Bride," "Mighty Mikko," "Devil's Hide" are some of the favorites.

The Wonder Clock and *Pepper and Salt.* Howard Pyle. Harper. The author, a great American writer and artist, was a lover of the old folk tales, and he wrote his stories in the old folk-tale pattern, some of them being almost a retelling with little touches all his own.

There are many many editions of Grimm's Fairy Tales but the loveliest for younger children, and the most beautiful telling is Wanda Gag's *Tales from Grimm.* Coward. She translated many stories before she made her final selection of those she thought most amusing for children. Her black-and-white pictures add to it greatly, too. It includes such favorites as "The Town Musicians of Bremen," "Cinderella," "Clever Elsie," "Cat and Mouse in Partnership." It is not as complete as the other Grimm's, but if you shut your eyes while someone is reading it you will hear the old grandmother telling the tales. Wanda Gag's *Snow White and the Seven Dwarfs* and *Gone is Gone: The Story of the Man Who Wanted to Do His Wife's Housework,* are equally delightful. One of the sad things of these times is that so many children think Walt Disney wrote "Snow White," and they do not know the utter delight of the original story.

Most of the familiar folk tales we know come from Grimm: "Rumplestiltskin," "Brave Little Tailor," "Little One Eye,

Little Two Eyes, Little Three Eyes," "Rapunzel," "Hare and Hedgehog," "Snow White and Rose Red," "Wolf and Seven Goats," "Golden Goose," "Sleeping Beauty," and many, many others not so well known. There are other Grimm's. One is stories selected by Eleanor Abbot, a lovely edition beautifully illustrated. Scribner.

Household Stories from the Collection of the Brothers Grimm. Translated from the German by Lucy Crane. Macmillan. A less expensive and very nice edition.

Surely every child should own his own Grimm. Wanda Gag's is the simplest for him to read to himself, and is a good beginning.

With Grimm we think of Hans Christian Andersen, only, I suppose, because they are both famous and every child should know them. The Grimm Brothers collected old folk tales that have been handed down for generations. Hans Christian Andersen wrote his own stories but they were influenced by the old folk tales. Many of Andersen's are too mature for children. They are "deep" and very sad. They are very beautiful. There are many editions of them. One of the best for children is *It's Perfectly True.* Translated by Paul Leyssac. Harcourt. This has twenty-eight stories by the Danish actor who has been telling them for years on radio. Favorites with the children are "The Tinder Box," "The Emperor's New Clothes," "The Princess and the Pea," "The Nightingale," "The Swineherd," "Little Claus and Big Claus."

There are many reprint editions, the best of which are: *Andersen's Fairy Tales.* Translated by Mrs. E. V. Lucas and Mrs. H. B. Paull. Grosset. *Andersen's Fairy Tales.* Illustrated by Jean O'Neill. World. They are quite complete and have nice type and illustrations

Some of the most charming stories are, of course, the Irish. The famous story-teller Seumas McManus made several collections: *The Donegal Wonder Book, Donegal Fairy Tales, In the Chimney Corner, Well o' The World's End.* Some of the favorite Irish stories are "Billy Beg and His Bull," "The Wee Red Man," "Hudden and Dudden and Donald O'Neary" (found in Joseph Jacob's *Celtic Tales*). They are not easy for children to read to themselves because of the twist in speech.

"Billy Beg and His Bull" is such a favorite with children. Once I was telling stories to a group of eleven-year-olds. A little Irish boy named Jerry said "Tell us Billy Beg and His Bull." The other children set up a howl. "Aw, Jerry, we know that story by heart." Jerry kept up his urging until finally I said, "Jerry, if you'll come to the library after school some night I'll tell it to you." Right away he came in. Could I tell it that night? I said, "Yes, and if you'd like to ask a few of your friends we might as well have more children." I promptly forgot about it, but strange things happened all day. Some children stopped by to ask how long the story hour would last. Parents called to see when it would be over. Other children wanted to know what stories I would tell. And so on. At three o'clock there was the most awful confusion outside of the library door. Over a hundred children stayed after school to hear "Billy Beg." I didn't know how many friends Jerry had.

Thirteen Danish Tales and *More Danish Tales*. Mary C. Hatch. Harcourt. Very amusingly written, and especially good for children to read to themselves.

Epaminondas and His Auntie. Sara Cone Bryant. Houghton. A classic story, and how little children love the little boy who had such difficulty getting things home that his auntie gave him, and the end where his mammy goes to auntie's herself, and says " 'There are five pies cooling on the steps. Be careful how you step in the pies.' And Epaminondas *was* careful. He stepped right in the middle of every single one. Now I wasn't there when his mammy came home so I don't know what happened. But I can guess." And the children all shout with such glee. "He got spanked!"

One of the most amusing and popular of the more recent collections of folk tales is *Once the Hodja*. Alice Geer Kelsey.

Longmans. Humorous tales from Turkey in which Nasred-Din Hodja, a simple fellow, gets in and out of trouble. There are, I am told, hundreds of Hodja stories, one for every occasion, and even in Turkey today someone will say something, and someone else will say "That reminds me of a Hodja story." They are liked by all children and grownups from about nine years on up. My favorite is "The Three Fridays." The book is very attractive, with nice illustrations and good type. It looks very readable. These are excellent for a mixed group of different ages and sexes.

Jack Tales and *Grandfather Tales.* Richard Chase. Houghton. Popular collections of American folk tales from North Carolina, Kentucky and Virginia. They are similar to European tales but have taken on a native humor of the regions whence they come. Ages 8-14.

Tales from Silver Lands. Charles Finger. Doubleday. Another Newbery book. These are South American tales that the author wrote down at first hand from the Indians' telling. Beautifully told, weird, with a real flavor of the country and people. "A Hungry Old Witch" is one of the best Hallowe'en stories I know. Good for all ages from eight up.

The Princess and the Goblins and *The Princess and Curdie.* George Macdonald. Macmillan Classics. Children of eight and up love to listen to them, and then reread them to themselves. A grownup reading these stories, unless he has experienced them himself, may think they are "dated," but once he tries them with children he will know how they love them, unusual words and all.

The Quaint and Curious Quest of Johnny Longfoot. Catherine Besterman. Bobbs. Based on an Old Polish tale, and a beautiful job of retelling. Johnny's father, a shoemaker, sends his son to visit his uncle who is a miser. Johnny goes in quest of seven-league boots and has many adventures. Eight-, nine-, ten-years-olds love this story.

Andrew Lang is one of the best known names in fairy tale

literature. For years, I am told, each Christmas a new Lang collection was published. *The Blue Fairy Book, Green Fairy Book, Red Fairy Book,* and so on. Longmans If one had a complete set of Lang's Fairy Books, that is about all he would need. He would have stories from many countries, he would have the best of Grimm, Andersen, *The Arabian Nights,* and many other classic stories. Most of them are now available in new editions with new illustrations and better print. In fact, when one looks at the contents of the first two, most of the stories you would like to have little children know are there. *Arabian Nights,* Andrew Lang. One of the best for children to own.

Myths are not as popular today as folk tales but many children love them, and more would, I am sure, if they were introduced to them.

The Wonder Book. Nathaniel Hawthorne. Houghton. Still one of the simplest tellings. The trouble with Hawthorne is that he uses the old device of stories within a story, and the framework is dated and not as interesting to children.

Adventures with the Gods. Catherine F. Sellew. Little. A more recent telling, and well liked by children, being readable-looking and not too difficult to read. It contains the best-know myths such as the ones about Pandora's box, Prometheus, Hercules, the miraculous pitcher, and a few others.

The Heroes, or Greek Fairy Tales. Charles Kingsley. Macmillan. Contains only stories about Perseus, the Argonauts, and Theseus, but it is still one of the best for they have been told with such vigor and beauty.

Recently there was published one of the most exciting and satisfying stories about the creation of the world: *Rise of the Thunderer* (Greek Mythology). Tom Galt, Crowell. It is told in a continuous story beginning before the beginning, so to speak. The gods are created, then man. Ten- and eleven-year-olds, and older, love this book. It has humor and beauty and suspense. It would be a good introduction to mythology for both boys and girls, and is wonderful to read to a group.

Of the Norse myths, one of the best for older boys and girls is Padraic Colum's *Children of Odin.* Macmillan. They are told in a running story in simple rhythmic prose. Ages 10-16.

Hero stories and legends are enjoyed by more children than myths, probably. Robin Hood is one of the most popular, and anyone can see why. For generations children have read about his daredevil exploits and played Robin Hood in the forest. There are many book about him, and your choice will be determined by the child for whom you are selecting it.

The Merry Adventures of Robin Hood of Great Renown in Nottinghamshire. Written and illustrated by Howard Pyle. Scribner. This is considered the best in style and for keeping the spirit of the old ballads. It is the most difficult to read but belongs in a child's library eventually, for it is the one he will want to keep all his life.

Robin Hood and His Merry Outlaws. J. W. McSpadden. Illustrated by Louis Slobodkin. World. This is a less expensive and a very attractive edition.

There are simpler versions of *Robin Hood* that are not so literary but often a boy who is not a very good reader or especially interested in reading will get his start with an easy Robin Hood.

King Arthur is another hero popular with children. Again, there are many editions.

The Story of King Arthur and his Knights. Howard Pyle. Scribner. One of the best, but it is one of the most difficult. There are three volumes to follow, making it one of the most complete. They are perfectly beautiful books to own. Ages 10-16.

The Book of King Arthur and His Noble Knights. Stories from Sir Thomas Malory's *Morte D'Arthur.* World. Faithful to the original spirit of the stories and much simpler to read, and shorter, than the Pyle or the famous Sydney Lanier's *King Arthur.*

Random House published in their Landmark Books a *King Arthur.* Dr. Mabel Robinson. While the language has not the beauty, nor is the spirit of the original stories as the above books, still to me it has real value. I have noticed how many children have read it who would not have read the other King Arthur books, simply because it is easier to read and looks so readable. This might well lead children to reading the more beautiful and difficult editions. Ages 9-14.

Other legendary heroes, popular with children, and tall-tale heroes, are Paul Bunyan and Pecos Bill.

Ol' Paul, The Mighty Logger. Written and illustrated by Glen Rounds. Holiday. Does not include the original stories of Paul's birth, but includes many new stories. It is a very funny, extremely well told, and especially popular with boys who are not too excited over reading as a pastime. It is a good starting place for a nonreader. Easy to read, too. The illustrations are very amusing. From this the youngster may well go to Esther Shepard's *Paul Bunyan.* Harcourt. Definitely for older children.

Pecos Bill and Lightning. Leigh Peck. Houghton. One of the best and the most fun of the stories about this legendary cowboy. This will suit the cowboy-loving boys from about eight years up.

Pecos Bill. James C. Bowman and Margery Bianco. Whitman. Entertaining for the older child, ages 10-16.

I haven't mentioned Bible stories for young people. Here are a few that children like especially:

The Golden Bible: From the King James version of the Old Testament. Selected and arranged by Elsa Jane Werner. Illustrated by Feodor Rojankovsky. Simon & Schuster. The spirit of the original was kept but vocabulary and phrasing are simplified. Lavishly illusrated. A large picture-book size book. Ages 8-14. Also *The Golden Bible: New Testament* in same format.

A Little Child. Text from New Testament selected by Jessie Orton Jones. Illustrated by Elizabeth Orton Jones.

Viking. The Christmas story beautifully illustrated with pictures of children in a school putting on a pageant. Children do like it. Ages 6-8.

The Christ Child. As told by Matthew and Luke, made by Maud and Miska Petersham. Doubleday. An interpretation with pictures of the spirit of the Holy Land which was the background of the childhood of Jesus. Ages 6-12.

Children of the Bible. Elizabeth Yates. Illustrated by Nora Unwin. Aladdin Books. An attractive little book telling of the boyhood of David, Samuel, Joseph, and others, ending with Jesus. Based on the King James version including some direct quotations. Ages 7-9.

Bible Stories for Boys and Girls: New Testament. Walter R. Bowie. Abingdon. A simple retelling of the story of Jesus and his followers by a great minister. Ages 10-16.

Rainbow Book of Bible Stories: Old Testament and New Testament. Mary Lamberton Becker. Illustrated by Hilda Van Stockum. World. Selected and arranged in chronological order to form a continuous narrative. Ages 9-12.

One God: The Ways We Worship Him. Florence Mary Fitch. Lothrop. Very popular, and about the only book of its kind on the different ways people worship—Catholics, Jews, Protestants. Ages 12-16.

Their Search for God: Ways of Worship in the Orient. Florence Mary Fitch. Lothrop. Not as popular as the other titles but a very interesting and useful book on Oriental religions. Ages 12-16.

VII

"The foolisher the better!"

FUNNY STORIES

"BUT PRINCESS, it's a very foolish story," said Stefan.

"The foolisher the better!" cried the Princess. And so, Stefan told the Princess the story that began "In my young days, when I was an old, old man . . ." which made the Princess laugh, and has made children laugh ever since. "So Stefan and the little Princess were married, and from that day the castle was no longer gloomy, but rang with laughter and merriment. Presently, the people of the kingdom, following the example of their rulers, were laughing too, and cracking jokes, and, strange to say, they soon found they were working all the better for their jollity."*

As Howard Pyle, the great American illustrator and writer of some of our classics for children said, "One must have a pinch of seasoning in this dull, heavy life of ours; one should never have all the troubles, the labors, the cares, with never a whit of innocent jollity and mirth. Yes, one must smile now and then, if for nothing else than to lift the corner of the lips in laughter that are all too often dragged down in sorrow."

Children, for the most part, adore funny stories. They

* Fillmore, Parker, *Mighty Mikko,* Harcourt.

adore pure nonsense. They love to laugh. The boy or girl who does not enjoy reading for reading's sake will usually "fall for" a funny book. The practical soul who delves in the mysteries of radio and "how to do it" books, will break down and read a *Freddy* book or *The Three Policemen,* or about the incomparable *Little Eddie.* Nonsense, either prose or poetry or a funny story is a good cement to join a group together, to start off a story hour, to unite a family.

As Mrs. Wiggins, the horse in the *Freddy* books, said, "Laughter destroys stuffed shirts." Do you remember the saying that if Will Rogers could have been sent to the Versailles Conference the results might have been different?

I had come back from a year off. A new boy, a round little boy, a stranger, came to me in my library. "I don't suppose you'd have the latest *Freddy* book?"

"What would you say if I have?" I parried, as I went to the shelf. Strange to say, it was there, and I handed it to him.

"I could *kiss* you," Paul exclaimed. Then he turned pink.

"You can skip the kissing until tomorrow," I said. The next day Paul sent his book back by *another* boy.

Yes, the *Freddy* books are to be reckoned with. There have been twenty-four of them, and the last one as much sought-after as the first. They are loved by all ages, from the littlest ones in school to those in Junior High, who don't mind a bit asking for them. Parents tell me they don't mind reading them aloud because they enjoy them so much themselves.

Freddy is a pig who lives on Mr. Bean's farm with the other animals. He is the only one who can read and is therefore infinitely superior. The animals have many adventures. There is quite a bit of satire which parents get as they read. That is why, I suppose, older people and older children enjoy them as much as the littlest ones.

Bill, about seven, came to the library to pick out his own book. He came up to the desk saying, "What I want is a good murder mystery." *Freddy the Detective* suited him to a T. No murder in it, just animals on Mr. Bean's farm and

Freddy, the pig who had been reading *Sherlock Holmes* and was doing a bit of sleuthing. Kurt Wiese's illustrations are almost worth "the price of admission." To see his pig with a Sherlock Holmes cap on, or in another book, Freddy in a cowboy suit, is *something*.

Riddles, cartoons, jokes, are popular with children. There have been a number of these the past few years, too.

One of the hardest things to do, of course, is to put yourself back as a little child and try to think what is funny. What seems funny to us now often is not funny to them. Doctor Dolittle seems funny to us but to some children he is a brave man and not a comic one.

Mary Poppins is an excruciatingly funny character to us, and yet, I can believe she is so real to many children, and they love her so, that they do not think of her as comic, although she makes them laugh. I know there are tears in children's eyes when she disappears at the end of each book.

The *Augustus* books make the children roar with laughter as he tries to fool his mother into not giving him a spring tonic, and then himself gets the dose of the awful stuff he fixes up. I doubt, however, if they know quite how funny Augustus is to grownups because we know him as a typical little boy. His logic makes grownups laugh. When Albert, his little friend, says you never see any pirates around, Augustus says quickly, "That is proof enough there are pirates, because if there were any you wouldn't see them." This is too much for Albert to follow.

The Peterkin Papers, printed first in 1890, is still a laugh maker. As Neill said when he brought the book back to the library after his mother had read it aloud to the family, "It even got a laugh out of Pop."

Little Eddie with his passion for collecting strange things; *Homer Price* and his doughnut machine, *Henry Huggins* and his dog, Ribsy, Geppy, the Striped Horse, who solved the circus mystery, *The Fabulous Flight, The Saucepan Journey,* to mention a few that are popular, are all books being read and laughed over today by all children.

" 'What nonsense!' the first lady-in-waiting murmured with a toss of her head.

'Yes, beautiful nonsense!' the Princess cried clapping her hands, and going off into peal after peal of merry laughter."

These books I am going to tell you about are *beautiful* nonsense, just the seasoning children need in their literary diet.

Favorite Funny Books

The Five Chinese Brothers. Claire Huchet Bishop. Illustrated by Kurt Wiese. Coward. A comical old folk tale retold with most amusing pictures to illustrate it. Five Brothers look exactly alike but each has a different gift. The first one is condemned to die. He is allowed to go home to say good-by to his mother. The second takes his place and uses his particular magic. Each in turn takes the place of the one before, and eventually the king gives up trying to kill them, and all ends well. Adults enjoy it too. All ages.

Curious George. Written and illustrated by H. S. Rey. Houghton. A very curious monkey is caught and brought to America. He gets into lots of trouble and gets out again. Children just *love* him. Ages 6-10. *Curious George Gets a Job* and *Curious George Rides a Bike* are equally good and amusing to all ages.

The Five Hundred Hats of Bartholomew Cubbins. Written and illustrated by Dr. Seuss (Theodore Geisel). Vanguard. When Bartholomew took off his hat respectfully to the king he found another hat, and another, and another, even as many as five hundred. No one could discover where they came from. This is a great favorite with the children. Other books by the same author are: *Scrambled Eggs Super, McElligot's Pool.*

Madeline. Written and illustrated by Ludwig Bemelmans. Simon & Schuster. Funny pictures and text tell about a little French girl in a Paris orphanage who has such a gay time with appendicitis that all the other little orphans get pains too. Almost adult, but children seem to think it is funny. *Madeline's Rescue,* a sequel (Viking), is just as funny. Ages 6-10.

The Pottlebys. Gertrude Crampton. Aladdin Books. An amusing and slightly stupid family (reminiscent of the Peterkins) have very ludicrous adventures in their daily life. Children love their crazy mistakes, such as the time they painted the sides of their house a different color—not intentionally, of course; and the time they planted the garden and forgot the seeds. These books are good for children to read to themselves. *Further Adventures of the Pottlebys* is a sequel. Ages 7-10.

Sophocles the Hyena. Jim Moran. Illustrated by Roger Duvoisin. McGraw. A cat named Morris convinced a dog, a duck, and a mole that they should go to cat school and learn to meow. Then a mean, hungry, cat-loving hyena appeared, and even Morris stopped meowing and tried to cock-a-doodle-do. From seven years on up, the children roar over this story and the pictures. Parents will enjoy the hidden meaning.

A Hero by Mistake. Anita Brenner. Illustrated by Charlot. Scott. Dionisia, an Indian, was afraid of almost everything. One day, unwittingly, he scared five bandits and then captured another with a price on his head. He became "Don Dionisio," and very rich. He was still afraid but he discovered that real courage was acting brave even if he was afraid. Very popular with all ages, a beautiful little book, and the story is beautifully told. Ages 8-14.

Freddy Goes to Florida. Walter R. Brooks. Illustrated by Kurt Wiese. Knopf. The first of a series of delightful nonsense about the animals on Mr. Bean's farm. Ages 5-15.

Not Really. Lesley Frost. Coward. Nonsense stories about a modern family who have strange adventures, such as getting caught up on a drawbridge, getting a giraffe for a pet, and other strange happenings. They are told in a very light and airy manner which seems to suit the stories. Seven- and eight-year-olds especially like them, and like to retell them to other children. Ages 7-10.

Don't Blame Me. Richard Hughes. Harper. This, and *Spider's Palace,* are very popular with eight- and nine-year-olds. They are nonsense stories, English in feeling, about such things as the large family of a king who live in a one-room palace on a rock, and what they do with all the children to keep them out from underfoot; and a little girl who went to live in a whale instead of Wales. Beautifully written and very funny for all ages. Good to read to a group of varied ages.

Pepper and Salt, or Seasoning for Young Folks. Written and illustrated by Howard Pyle. Harper. A retelling of old folk tales with Pyle's special brand of humor, and his own particular little twist to the plots. "Clever Peter and the Two Bottles" is a favorite with little children. *The Wonder Clock* is another wonderful collection by the same author. Both of these books should be in every child's library. They will be read again and again. They are already classics. Ages 6-12.

The Peterkin Papers. Lucretia Hale. Houghton. Although written in 1874 for St. Nicholas Magazine, these stories are timeless. Twenty-two stories about the stupid Peterkins who try to become wise and get into strange difficulties from which they are saved by the common sense of The Lady from Philadelphia. As one youngster said of her, "The Lady from Philadelphia was not really so smart. The Peterkins were so stupid." Belongs on every family bookshelf. Extremely popular. Ages 8-14.

Mr. Popper's Penguins. Richard and Florence Atwater. Illustrated by Robert Lawson. Little. Mr. Popper, a mild little house painter with a love of Polar exploration, was presented with a penguin that he named Captain Cook. In order to make the penguin happy the Poppers had to do many unusual things, such as putting a handle *inside* of the refrigerator door so the penguin could let himself out, and flooding and freezing the basement for Captain Cook's plea-sure. Because Captain Cook was lonely the zoo sent them Greta, another penguin. Soon there was a family of penguins. Life became quite different for the Poppers. They traveled around showing their trained penguins. Everybody, from six to sixty, loves this book. Every child *must* know it.

Augustus and the River. Written and illustrated by Le-Grand. Bobbs. Another series the children will read right through. Ten-year-old Augustus lived on a shanty boat with his parents and brother and sister. They had uproarious times in their everyday life on the boat. Pa and Ma are just as ludicrous as the children. The speech is full of quaint expressions that children remember and use—"Fry me for a catfish," and such. *Augustus Goes South, Augustus in the Mountains,* and others. Ages 7-14.

Miss Pickerell Goes to Mars. Ellen MacGregor. McGraw. Miss Pickerell is one of the funniest characters, and both boys and girls love to follow her crazy adventures. When she returns from a vacation she finds a large rocketship in her pasture. By accident she takes off on the rocketship with the crew and goes to Mars. Three other stories about her: *Miss Pickerell and the Geiger Counter, Miss Pickerell Goes Undersea, Miss Pickerell Goes to the Arctic.* Ages 8-14.

Once the Hodja. Alice Geer Kelsey. Illustrated by Frank Dobias. Longmans. Funny Turkish folk tales retold. Nasred-Din-Hodja, simple and kindly, is both wise and foolish. He gets into many scrapes and gets out of them again. A very attractive little book that the whole family will enjoy reading and listening to. Ages 8 and up.

Time to Laugh. Stories selected by Phyllis Fenner. Illu-strated by Henry Pitz. Knopf. A collection of funny stories from folk tales and modern stories. Children like it, and it is especially good for reading aloud to all ages. Ages 8-12. Other funny books by the same author: *Fools and Funny Fellows, Gigglebox, Fun Fun Fun.*

Here Comes Kristie. Written and illustrated by Emma

Brock. Knopf. A very funny story about two boys who pool their money and buy a horse that turns out to be temperamental. Children find this book not only easy to read but a good story. Others by the same author: *Kristie and the Colt, The Plughorse Derby* (an amusing story of a little girl who races the plow horse and wins by whispering "oats" in the horse's ear).

The Great Geppy. Written and illustrated by William Pene DuBois. Viking. In which the mysterious disappearance of the circus money is solved by Geppy, the striped horse. A very unusual, funny and useful mystery. Useful because many boys who don't like to read will read this one. Others equally popular with the same crowd: *The Three Policemen, Peter Graves, Twenty One Balloons, The Giant. My Father's Dragon*. Ruth S. Gannett. Illustrated by Ruth Chrisman Gannett. Random House. A little boy rescues a baby dragon from a Wild Island inhabited by fierce animals. A delightful, crazy bit of nonsense that children take to. Sequel: *Elmer and the Dragon*. Ages 8-12.

Honk the Moose. Phil Strong. Illustrated by Kurt Wiese. Dodd. Great excitement and doings when two Minnesota boys discover a moose in the stable. Others by the same author: *Way Down Cellar, Captain Kidd's Cow, Censored the Goat*. Ages 8-14.

Tyll Ulenspiegel's Merry Pranks. M. Jagendorf. Illustrated by Fritz Eichenberg. Vanguard. Thirty-seven stories of the funny legendary character, Tyll. Tyll plays jokes on his enemies but helps the poor and good. Every child should know Tyll. As one child wrote about him, "This is a book full of the funniest tales ever a man has written. Tyll was a man that believed in laughter and merry pranks and this book is certainly full of them." Another book equally amusing and readable by the same author is *Merry Men of Gotham*. Ages 8-14.

The Poetic Parrot. Margaret Mackay. Day. A parrot, who talks in rhyme, escapes from the zoo and has many adventures, among them catching burglars in a pet shop. A very unusual, modern, funny story, easy to read, and good to read aloud. As Betsy, nine years old, wrote, "I think this is a good book because it has so much humor, I enjoyed the excitement but at the same time it was quite funny. One thing that made it funny was the fresh things the parrot said." Both boys and girls like it. Ages 8-12.

Lion in the Woods. Maurice Dolbier. Little. The animals are led to believe that there is a lion prowling in their woods. Everybody believes the newspaper headlines and think they see the lion. It is called a "fable for today." Excruciatingly funny to children. Ages 8-12.

The Cello in the Belly of the Plane. Joseph Schrank. Watts. When the airplane in which the boy was riding was about to make a forced landing he becomes a hero by playing the three pieces he knows on his 'cello. Uproariously funny. Ages 5-10.

Little Eddie. Written and illustrated by Carolyn Haywood. Morrow. One of the rarest characters is the incomparable Eddie, who collects everything he can find. Children love him. There are several very funny books about him: *Eddie and the Fire Engine, Eddie and Gardenia, Eddie's Pay Dirt, Eddie and His Big Deals.* Ages 7-12.

Ben and Me. A new and astonishing life of Benjamin Franklin as written by his good mouse, Amos; lately discovered, edited and illustrated by Robert Lawson. Little. Amos was the mouse who lived in Franklin's cap. Everywhere Franklin went Amos went, too. His diary tells a humorous life of Benjamin Franklin with all the well-known episodes seen from the viewpoint of Amos. A very clever story, liked by children of different ages. Other funny books by this same author-artist: *The Fabulous Flight* (in which a boy grows smaller instead of bigger); *McWhinney's Jaunt; Mr. Wilmer.* All are popular and all are beautifully illustrated with Mr. Lawson's black-and-white drawings. Ages 8-14.

Alphonse the Bearded One. Natalie Carlson. Illustrated

by Nicholas. Harcourt. A Canadian folk tale of a bear cub trained by his master to be a soldier. When his master is conscripted to fight against the Indians, he sends Alphonse in his place, and Alphonse succeeds very well as a soldier and a spy. Hilarious reading! Ages 8-14.

Homer Price. Written and illustrated by Robert McCloskey. Viking. Six funny stories about Homer, his aunts and uncles and his neighbors who live in Centerburg. One of the most popular stories is about the doughnut machine that won't stop and makes hundreds of doughnuts. Every child should know Homer Price. Boys and girls from seven up will enjoy hearing and reading about him. The illustrations are perfect. Ages 7-14.

The Little Witch. Ann Bennett. Lippincott. A very unusual story of a nine-year-old child of a witch who wants to go to school and have friends like other children rather than mix the Black Spell Brew and ride at night on a broomstick. When she goes to school she takes her broomstick with her and gives the children rides. When she mixes some of the brew and turns the children into flowers the readers love it. Ages 8-12.

Henry Huggins. Beverly Cleary. Morrow. Henry gets himself into lots of funny situations in this and the books that follow it: *Henry and Ribsy, Henry and Beezus, Otis Spoffard.* Ages 8-12.

Herbert. Hazel Wilson. Knopf. Herbert is full of ideas, most of which get out of control. Each chapter is hilarious adventure with him, his zoo, his chemical experiments, his collecting can tops, his desert island. Two other Herbert books: *Herbert Again,* and *More Herbert.*

Billy Had a System. Marion Hollands. Knopf. Billy and his friend, Fatso, have a number of harrowing experiences that are very funny. The funniest, from which the book gets its name, is about the system Billy had for getting prizes at birthday parties, and how he and Fatso end up with the birthday cake. A sequel is *Billy's Club House.* Ages 8-12.

Mary Poppins. P. L. Travers. Illustrated by Mary Shepard. Harcourt. It is hard to know whether to put this with funny books or fantasy. Certainly it is very funny and children adore it. As one girl wrote, "It is a hilarious comedy about a woman who acts very queerly, but can be nice. She has many unusual adventures which can lead to trouble. Jane is one of the Banks children in the story. She is sorry she is the oldest. The twins are sometimes quiet and sometimes noisy. Michael is inquisitive. And it all leads up to a lot of fun. It has some nice illustrations which nearly always make you laugh."

The time Mary Poppins took laughing gas and floated up near the ceiling is an incident children never forget. The science teacher had been teaching the law of gravity to a second grade. When she came in for the next lesson, one of the children showed her a picture of Mary Poppins floating around, saying, "There goes your laws of gravity, Miss Nichols." It is one of the great books of our time, and every child should have the three books: *Mary Poppins Opens the Door* and *Mary Poppins Comes Back.* Ages 5-12.

Pay Dirt. Written and illustrated by Glen Rounds. Holiday. "The story of how Uncle Torwal and Whitey had left their ranch to sluice for gold in the Black Hills because of drought and too many grasshoppers. I liked the story very much because it was humorous and at the same time informative." And the girl who wrote that hits it right. It is one of the funniest of stories, and at the same time there is a lot of information about gold sluicing. Ages 8-16. Excellent for the older boy who thinks he doesn't like reading.

First Book of Jokes and Funny things. Frances Chrystie. Watts. Funny stories and funny pictures.

Jokes, Jokes, Jokes. Collected by Helen Hoke. Watts. All kinds of funny stories, old and new. A big book full of laughs. Ages 9-12.

Riddle Me This. Frances Chrystie. Oxford. A little book of riddles that interest little children. Ages 7-9.

First Book of Cartoons for Kids. Selected by children with the help of Phyllis Fenner. Watts. Favorite cartoons chosen by children themselves. Ages 6-12.

The books of funny poems are listed with poetry but just to name them: *Tirra Lirra,* by Laura E. Richards, Little, just out in a new edition; *The Complete Nonsense Book,* by Edward Lear, Dodd, a classic that every home should have; *A Rocket in My Pocket,* edited by Carl Withers, Holt, the rhymes and chants of young Americans; *Yours Till Niagara Falls,* compiled by Lillian Morrison, Crowell, things written in autograph books; *Jonathan Bing,* by Beatrice Curtis Brown, Oxford, rhymes about absent-minded old gentlemen who had lots of difficulties.

VIII

"*If you're normal . . .*"

ADVENTURE STORIES

"GUESS WHAT I'VE GOT this time!" wrote the ten-year-old book reviewer. *Who rides in the Dark.* It really is swell. *If you're normal* you'll just thrill to Dan's meeting with the mysterious person who calls himself Captain Hairtrigger, and if you know a good book when you read one you'll just love the places where Dan stops the mysterious intruder from robbing the till. Try to get it. It's written by Stephen Meader."

There are some authors who seem to know the perfect recipe for good adventure stories, and Stephen Meader is one of them.

What is an adventure book? What is adventure?

"Take the Adventure, heed the call, now ere the irrevocable moment passes! 'Tis but a banging of the door behind you, a blithesome step forward, and you are out of the old life and into the new!"*

"Adventure," says the dictionary, "an exciting or unusual experience." What may be adventure for one is not for another. An adventure for a five-year-old may be a walk down the street.

One nice thing about adventure is that it can come to anyone. It can happen anywhere, at any time, in your backyard, or in faraway places. It can be quiet adventure or one

* Grahame, Kenneth, *The Wind in the Willows,* Scribner.

in which you meet strange peoples and there are mysterious doings. You can't choose the kind of adventure you'll meet but you can choose the kind of adventure you read about. That makes books seem all the more wonderful.

Children, like the rest of us, need vicarious adventure. Many kinds of adventure can be had only in books.

What is the recipe for a good adventure story? What is it that Stephen Meader, Jim Kjelgaard, William Steel, Kate Seredy, Carolyn Haywood, Clyde Bulla have, just to mention a few who know the proper ingredients?

May Lamberton Becker, an authority on the subject, says, "In all good adventure stories something must not only happen but keep on happening. The narrative should be kept buzzing along by events rather than under rhetorical pressure."

The children back her up in that. Years ago Alex, who read more books than almost anyone I know, returned two books he had had for the week end. One shall be nameless but was by an author well thought of by librarians, and the other was *Shadow in the Pines* by Stephen Meader (also well thought of by librarians, I hasten to add). Alex tried to explain to me why he liked the Meader book better. Finally, he said, "Here, I'll show you" and he read from the two books. The one began with two or three pages of description, but Meader's began with a boy and a dog in the woods. Action right away, and yet, within a short space of time, the atmosphere was firmly established. I once had the pleasant experience of reading that book aloud. It is a good test of the quality of a book to listen to it read aloud. Surely there is no harm in a good beginning.

Listen to what many other children say about books. Harry, an excellent reader, said, when I asked him to try a book for me, "I read through the fourth chapter. . . . Let me put it this way, I've learned this about most books, the first three chapters are *nothing*." Harry was a good enough reader so he could read the first three or four chapters before giving up. Many children are not. As a girl said about a book, "I don't like a book that starts out dull because some people may not give it a chance and just put it back where they got it. I think to make a book interesting it must have a good plot and it must have a story that is easy to understand."

"Exciting right from the beginning, which most books are not," said someone about *Down the Big River.*

Sometimes the reverse is true, a book does not live up to its good beginning. A youngster wrote this: "At the beginning of the book I thought that I would enjoy it a great deal, but after I read the first two and one-half chapters I gave up. After the first chapter I started to lose the story, and then after the second chapter I completely lost the story."

Of Maristan Chapman's mysteries someone said, "I have read a lot of Mr. Chapman's books, and every time you start to read one you want to read it over and over again." Pretty good for a mystery!

"All his books are good," the ten-year-old said of Jim Kjelgaard's books, "the working, the story, the good-size print, just everything good."

Good beginnings, then, are part of the recipe.

Titles play quite a part in what children read, too. Some titles do not mean anything. If each book could be handed personally by some enthusiastic admirer to a child, and the title explained, or the book read without reference to the title, that would be different. But when there are hundreds of books on the library shelves, and sometimes a very short time in which to select a book, the books with very literary titles, or strange names that convey nothing, are passed by. The same is probably true in a book shop unless the salesman knows his stock and has enthusiasm for what he sells.

As Joan said about a book, "The title of the book doesn't sound interesting, and most people read the first page to see if the book is good, and the first page is the dullest page in the first chapter, and the first chapter is boring and dull." She settled that book for good and all.

"I just finished the book *Open Daily,*" wrote Carolyn. "I think the book is very good. Most of this book is funny. The reason the people have not read it is probably because of the title. The title isn't very interesting and I think that's the reason why nobody has read it. And you wouldn't think it was about a zoo."

We don't have to worry about the avid readers who will read anything in print. It is the children who are not good readers or particularly interested in reading who get bogged down. I am sure there are many adults the same way. The speedy reader slithers through a great deal of description and atmosphere and comment to get to the action (like Harry and his first three chapters that he expected to be dull). A poorer, less mature reader cannot do it. And a child, not-too-eager, when looking for a book will take the obvious title like *The Mystery in the Old Red Barn* instead of *Treasure Was Their Quest,* or *An Ear for Uncle Emil,* which mean nothing unless you read the books.

"When you first read *Way Down Cellar* it seems uninteresting until page twenty-nine, then the story gets funny, mysterious and interesting. I recommend it for those from six to sixty. My mother read it too, although she isn't fifty. In my mind it is a very good book." In other words, that book had a universal quality.

Another thing mentioned was "good print." With younger children the looks of a book is very important. Children take a look at a page of type and it "makes or breaks" them. Too often, when it is a large-sized book, and there is a whole page of text unbroken by pictures and badly spaced, the child who doesn't read too easily says "It is too hard" before he has even read a word. I can think of many really good stories that discourage children just by their looks. And I can think of many books that the children "go for" largely because they look so readable. A mother once complained to me that her children would not read the books that were in their father's library, yet they would bring home *The Jungle Book,* and similar older books, from the school library. I knew why it was. The father's editions were the older ones with few illustrations and bad print and spacing.

Good beginnings, good title, universal quality, good type and spacing. What else makes a book readable to a child?

Karl, who wasn't much interested in literature but mostly in boats, made a very astute remark about *Treasure Island.* "He [Stevenson] *makes it a point to be exciting.*" Stevenson was trying to tell a good story, to interest children, particularly his own stepson for whom he was writing it.

Another child writes "I like to find mystery and suspence or exciting *advenchers* or comical stories in a book. I think these things are what make good books. If the books I read don't have some one of these things I find them dull. I don't like books that have a lot of explaining or slow moving; if they are like that I most always don't finish them."

A little girl made a really terrific remark, and maybe her idea has more to do with what makes books interesting than anything else considered. Said she, "It sounded like the writer was having lots of fun."

Book characters should seem real and be consistent. Wrote Bill, "*Hudson Bay Express* is a good title for this book for it is full to the brim with adventure and danger always connected with the Hudson Bay region of the north. The book is exciting and fast moving with short chapters which do not end at the most exciting part of the adventure. . . . The only thing wrong with it is that it's hard to believe that two boys could have so many adventures."

"One of my favorite books," wrote Jacqueline, "is *The Singing Tree.* I like it because it seemed so very real and the characters seemed to always do something. I also thought I would have to finish it before putting it down."

George wrote about *Steppin and Family,* "I like this book because Steppin had some troubles and everything wasn't alright the way some books are. The only thing I thought was wrong is that people don't give away pianos."

The height, of course, is reached in the comment about one of Elizabeth Coatsworth's books: "I like the *hole* story."

Mrs. Becker in her very helpful book *Adventures in Reading,* Lippincott, says that the three tests of a good book for children are, "Sincerity, vitality, and a technique that is adequate." Honesty and sincerity of purpose, joy in doing it; background and characters real; a technique (good beginnings, and all the rest) adequate for children for whom they are written.

Seldom does an author who has a lesson to teach, whether it be morals or geography, write a book that is really interesting to children. The story must be the important thing. In these days of getting acquainted with our far-off neighbors, many books have been written having to do with children of other climates and customs. Few of them, from the child's point of view, have been successful. A person with something to teach is too conscious of the lesson, and the story suffers. It is only when a writer has a story that really must be told, and it just happens to be in a foreign setting, that the book is popular, like *The Good Master.* One can learn more about the customs of Hungary through that book than from many others in which the authors have tried to teach. *The Hundred Dresses* is a better teacher of behavior toward others, because Eleanor Estes has a story to tell, than a book where the author had primarily a lesson to teach without feeling the story. When I read her story to some twelve-year-olds and was a bit self-conscious about so much mental action, I said, "Weren't you a little bored when that little girl worried in the night?" "I worried right with her," said one of the boys.

People who have tried to teach nature study, scientific facts, facts about life in other countries through a feeble story around made-up characters have not been successful because children do not read the books. They like their facts to be straight, their story to be good. In a new book, *Lions in the Woodshed* by Margaret J. Baker, a story having to do with some very real children, there is this passage that is also very real, from a boy's point of view: "Most of the books behind the locked doors were tales that pretended to be stories but which really only concealed useful facts about natural history, and how a gas meter works, and the children in them had scientific elder brothers who were content to spend whole Saturday afternoons answering intelligent questions." So, you see, the children are "on to" those little tricks of covering facts with story. And they don't want it that way. They hate to have the authors think they are fooling them.

Adventure for little children needs very little plot, but what there is does have to be scaled to the little child. *Little Tim and the Brave Sea Captain,* for example, or *Two Cars,* in which an old-fashioned car and a new car race against each other. Usually children like to read about slightly older children than themselves. Little Tim seems to be the exception, for he is only five. *Little Steam Roller* is another exciting adventure for the six-year-old. *Looking for Something* is a charming adventure of a little burro.

There are many kinds of adventure books, and anyone may take his pick. Children are likely to "go hard" on one kind for a while, and then switch to another kind.

The covered wagon stories are not as popular as they once were, perhaps because there have not been as many lately. There is a variation in *Sheep Wagon Family.* Indian stories are not as much in demand today as modern adventure. Cowboy books are still pretty popular, especially with the little fellows, and there are many modern ranch stories, read almost more by girls than boys. The cowboy adventures range all the way from *Cowboy Small* for the littlest to *Lone Cowboy* for the older ones. There are many easy-to-read stories about cowboys and horses and they are a help for the older children who are having reading troubles.

Stories with historic background have been losing out somewhat unless they are unusually good, like *Johnny Tremain, Green Cockade,* and some for younger children.

Space stories were in great demand by both boys and girls

a couple of years ago but the excitement has subsided somewhat. The good ones still go. So far there have not been too many really good space story books. For the little fellow there have been three really topnotch stories: *The Magic Ball from Mars,* a combination of fact and fantasy that children from eight years up love; *Space Ship Under the Apple Tree,* in which a man from Mars comes to earth and learns about us; *Space Cat,* a charming story in which a kitten goes to the moon with a young aviator. *Freddy and the Space Ship,* and *Freddy and the Men from Mars,* and *Miss Pickerell Goes to Mars* are comical stories and can't be considered in the class of space stories. *The Wonderful Flight to the Mushroom Planet* is one of the best for the eights to twelves, a fine story with real boys and good adventure.

The largest groups of adventure books, of course, are everyday adventure (individuals and families), and mysteries. There seems to be some feeling on the part of parents that mysteries are bad for children. I would ask, what mysteries? For a good mystery is just as good as any good adventure story, and a bad one is just as bad, and no worse, than another kind of adventure that is poorly written. Mysteries for children usually have very slight mystery, just enough to give suspense for a youngster. Sometimes it seems that about the only mystery is in the title. Children love suspense but more than that they love to read what their mothers and fathers are reading. With the exception of a few books for older boys, there is seldom, if ever, a murder in a child's story. The mysteries involve things disappearing, ghosts that turn out to be squirrels in the attic, buried treasure, poaching, and "crimes" that a child might solve himself. The best mystery I ever read for children, I think, was *The Stranger in Primrose Lane,* a spy story of England during the last war. Helen Fuller Orton's mysteries entrance the children, not because they are terribly exciting, or because of their literary quality, but because they are about children like themselves and the children in the story solve the mysteries that they themselves might solve.

Some mysteries for youngsters are highly amusing, such as a recent one, *The Dagger, the Fish and Casey McKee,* which is a good peppy mystery with lots of fun.

Sherlock Holmes is not too adult for the older boys and girls, and there is a special edition, *Boys' Sherlock Holmes,* which contains those stories most suited, most interesting, to the young people.

The Father Brown stories, by G. K. Chesterton, in which a rosy cheeked little priest solves the mysteries, is another collection for older children.

A mystery book will sometimes lead a child to read for fun when he had not been inclined that way. The easy-to-read Orton mysteries and those of Mary Graham Bonner not only give a child the reading practice he needs, but the pleasure that comes from reading. And isn't he reading a mystery just like Daddy?

Everyday adventure books include almost everything from *Billy and Betsy* to *The Boy Who Stole the Elephant* or *Train For Tiger Lily.* They are about everyday kids in everyday settings. That something unusual usually happens is the adventure.

As I said before, what is exciting to one is not to another. To the little girl a story about a canary was very "exciting." But the joy is, each can select his own. Here are some suggestions for good "advenchers."

Favorite Adventure Stories

Tim to the Rescue. Written and illustrated by Edward Ardizzone. Oxford. Little Tim of *Little Tim and the Brave Sea Captain* has another adventure when he rescues Ginger, the ship's boy, in a terrific hurricane, thereby reforming Ginger and getting a gold medal for himself. Real adventure for the youngest.

Little Old Automobile. Written and illustrated by Marie

Hall Ets. Viking. Little Old Automobile says, "I won't" just once too often and received his comeuppance. Four- to seven-year-olds thoroughly relish the humor. (*In the Forest, Mr. T. W. Anthony Woo, Another Day,* by the same author.)

Two Cars. Written and illustrated by Ingri and Edgar d'Aulaire. Doubleday. An amusing race between a shiny new car and a battered old one. A new version of the hare and the tortoise. The pictures are wonderful. Ages 4-8.

Little Steam Roller. Grahame Green. Lothrop. Setting, London Airport. The plot concerns some wicked smugglers and how the steam roller is instrumental in capturing them. Ages 5-8.

Country Garage. Jerrold Beim. Morrow. A little boy helps his uncle in his service station. Ages 5-8.

Looking for Something. Ann Nolan Clark. Illustrated by Leo Politi. Viking. An inquisitive little gray burrow wanders from place to place looking for something. He finally finds something that is for him alone. Ages 5-8.

Pet of the Met. Written and illustrated by Lydia and Don Freeman. Viking. A white mouse and his family lived in an attic of the opera house. He was a lover of music and helped turn the pages for the prompter. There also lived in the basement of the Met a cat, Mefisto. How the two became acquainted and resolved their difficulties is an amusing story with lovely pictures. Ages 5-8.

The Poppy Seeds. Clyde Bulla. Illustrated by Jean Charlot. Crowell. How a little Mexican boy planted poppy seeds, and through them happiness and good will were brought to his people. Ages 5-8.

Magic Money. Ann Nolan Clark. Illustrated by Lee Politi. Viking. Tony, a young Costa Rican boy, wanted to earn money to buy his grandfather two white oxen. His grandfather finally thought of a way to earn it. Children love this story. Ages 5-8.

Andy and the Lion. Written and illustrated by James Daugherty. Viking. Andy was a small boy with a passion for lions, so he went to the library for a book about them. He finally dreamed about them. On his way to school the next morning what should he meet but a lion with a thorn in his paw. Later when the circus came to town the lion recognized him. A tall tale that is a classic already. Ages. 5-9.

Burma Boy. Willis Lindquist. Pictures by Nicolas Mordvinoff. McGraw. Haji loved the mighty elephant, Madja Koom, and when he disappeared, Haji went in search of him. There is suspense in this story and great beauty in the telling. Ages 8-10.

Chinese Children Next Door. Pearl Buck. Day. At bedtime an American mother tells her four little children of her childhood in China, and especially about the Chinese family who lived next door. A really charming story telling of the customs in China. Ages 6-8. Other titles by the same author: *The Big Wave, Dragon Fish, Water-buffalo Children.*

Lucky Days for Johnny. Irene Smith. Illustrated by Kurt Wiese. McGraw. An everyday story of a small boy, his teacher and his family. When his teacher came for dinner Friday night he had a wonderful time. A great favorite with children. Ages 7-10.

Little Pear. Written and illustrated by Eleanor Lattimore. Harcourt. A small boy called to me on the street one day, "Hi, Miss Fenner, I just finished reading *Litter Pear,* and was it mel-LOW, oh boy!" I never see that book without thinking "Mel-LOW, oh boy." It has been a favorite for many years, this story of a mischievous five-year-old Chinese boy who had many adventures, some not so pleasant. Ages 6-8. Other books by the same author: *Wu, The Gatekeeper's Son, Little Pear and His Friends, Diana of the China Shop.*

B is for Betsy. Written and illustrated by Carolyn Haywood. Harcourt. Betsy's experiences during the first year of school and vacation on her grandfather's farm. The adventures are such as any child might have and children, boys and girls, love all of the Betsy books. Other titles: *Back to School with Betsy, Betsy and Billy, Betsy and the Boys, Betsy's*

Little Star, Primrose Day, Betsy and the Circus, Here's a Penny, and others. A real "must" for children just beginning to enjoy reading. They are simply told with a great deal of humor, and look so readable. Ages 7-10.

Cinders. Katherine Gibson. Illustrated by Vera Bock. Longmans. Who was the little man in the grey coat? He couldn't remember himself. He had a way with horses, loved cheese. This is a fairy tale, a war story, a horse story; in fact, it is any kind of a story a child would like. It is beautifully told, exciting, easy to read, and a cute little book that every child should know. "They didn't know I was afraid," said Cinders, "and that was almost as good as being really truly brave." Another by the same author: *Oak Tree House.*

Tag-along Tooloo. Frances Clark Sayers. Illustrated by Helen Sewell. Viking. Tooloo was five and a nuisance to her older sister for she wanted to do everything *she* did. When she couldn't she got into mischief by copying her. A delightful story for little girls especially. I was walking along the corridor once and I heard some little girls singing behind me: "We are Tag-along Tooloos. We are Tag-along Tooloos." Ages 7-10.

Space Ship Under the Apple Tree. Written and illustrated by Louis Slobodkin. Macmillan. A little man from Mars comes down to earth and learns about us. Ages 6-10.

Space Cat. Ruthven Todd. Scribner. An ambitious young cat, Flyball, goes off in a rocket with his master and has super adventures. Ages 7-10.

The Boy Who Stole the Elephant. Julilly H. Kohler. Knopf. When Gyp, who worked for a one-horse circus, heard a plot to sell the elephant that he cared for, he stole it. If you can imagine trying to "get away" with an elephant in Ohio you'll know how crazy it was. All turned out well for everybody but the villain. Ages 8-10.

Little House in the Big Woods. Laura Ingalls Wilder. Illustrated by Garth Williams. Harper. Of all the many books published in the last twenty years the books in this series probably mean more to more people than any others. They are based on Mrs. Wilder's childhood, as accurately as she could remember. And what a life it was! Beginning with this book, pioneer life in Wisconsin, with blizzards, wolves, lack of comforts, the series goes from one frontier to the next with all the experiences that went with them. She has made the family so real that children feel as if they knew them each personally. They are written in the third person, and as one child said, "Wasn't Mrs. Wilder smart. She didn't say I all the time." Children read these books again and again. They are the kind of books to own . . . definitely! Other titles in the same series are: *Little House on the Pairie, On the Banks of Plum Creek, Long Winter, By the Shores of Silver Lake, Little Town on the Pairie, Farmer Boy, Those Happy Golden Years.* They are out in a fine new edition with lovely illustrations. Ages 8-14.

The Swiss Family Robinson. Johann D. Wyss. Macmillan. There are many editions of this classic. There are two less expensive editions, one published by Grosset and one by World Publishing Company, but since it is a book most children will want to keep forever, it would be a good idea to have the best.

Still one of the most popular of the old books. Of course, it is impossible, this tale of a family shipwrecked on a desert island—all the things that happen to them, the varieties of animals and plants in the same spot—but that makes it all the more delightful. There is something about people scrabbling for a living in a remote place, the details of daily life, that fascinates children. There is great reality in this unreal tale. Ages 8-12.

The Five Little Peppers and How They Grew. Margaret Sidney. Grosset. This story of a delightful family, with so little to do with but lots of family love, still interests children. It has outlived many similar series of its time. Who will ever forget Polly, Joel, Dave and Phronsie, the broken down stove and their fun with simple things? *Five Little Peppers Midway, Five Little Peppers Grown Up,* etc. Ages 8-12.

The Trolley Car Family. Eleanor Clymer. McKay. A

modern Five Little Peppers. A delightful family move to the country for the summer and live in a trolley car their father had driven. Children adore the fixing up of the car for living, and the "advencher" is good. Ages 8-12.

The Saucepan Journey. Edith Unnerstad. Macmillan. Translated from the Swedish. A very amusing story of the Larssons and their seven children who, not having room in their small apartment for all of them (the baby slept in the bureau drawer), started out in a wonderful caravan contrived by the father who was quite an inventor. On the way they sold his marvelous singing saucepan. They had an exciting trip full of happenings and found a larger place in which to live. Excellent for reading aloud. Ages 8-12.

Twenty and Ten. As told by Janet Joly. By Claire Huchet Bishop. Illustrated by William Pene DuBois. Viking. A magnificent story which takes place during the occupation of France by the Nazis, when twenty French children, all about ten years old, except for the little brother of one of them, go to the mountains in charge of a Sister. To their school came ten refugee children to be hidden from the enemy. The way the children connive to hide their guests and outwit the Nazis is a great story. It is written as if told by one of the children. How children enjoy hearing it! They are breathless with suspense, and laugh out loud when the children fool the enemy. I think I have never read a story to a group (all ages) that had such a reception. And then, the children read it all over to themselves. It takes only an hour to read the whole story. It would be a fine experience for a family group to share.

The Good Master. Written and illustrated by Kate Seredy. Viking. Lively and naughty Kate goes from Budapest to live on her uncle's farm. There is a great deal of fun and also serious charm in the way the uncle, "the good master," "gentles" Kate. An authentic story of customs on the Hungarian plains. Children who like horse stories will enjoy it too. Sequel to it: *The Singing Tree.* These books are well on their way to being classics. Ages 8-12. Other books by the same author: *A Tree for Peter, Open Gate, Chestry Oak.*

The Melendy Family. Written and illustrated by Elizabeth Enright. Rinehart. A very modern motherless family of two boys and two girls, with a very understanding father and a wonderful housekeeper, in the first book, *The Saturdays,* have a wonderful idea of what to do with their Saturdays in New York. They pool their spending money and take turns having just the kind of time each wants. In the succeeding books, the family has adventures in the country. Children adore these stories. Ages 9-12. Three books in one. Also published separately as: *The Saturdays, Four Story Mistake, And Then There Were Five.*

Door in the Wall. Written and illustrated by Marguerite DeAngeli. Doubleday. The dramatic story of Robin, the crippled son of a great lord in thirteenth century England, who overcame his disabilities by craftsmanship and eventually won his knighthood by a courageous act. Won the Newbery Award. Ages 8-12. Other titles by same author: *Coppertoed Boots, Three, Hannah, Up the Hill.*

The Cottage at Bantry Bay. Written and illustrated by Hilda Van Stockum. Viking. An utterly delightful Irish family has very wonderful adventures and find a treasure which is a great help to them. The warmth of the family, the humor and the really good plot make this a very good and popular book. *Francie on the Run* follows this story, in which six-year-old Francie runs away from the hospital where he has had an operation on his foot, and has many adventures getting home. Beautifully told. *Pegeen,* by the same author, tells of a very small and very lively Irish girl who comes to live with the O'Sullivan's. Other books by the same author that children adore are about an American family: *The Mitchells,* followed by their further adventures in *Canadian Summer.* Ages 10-14.

Bright Days. Written and illustrated by Madye Chastain. Harcourt. The Fripsey family moving next door quite changed Marcy's life. Never had she seen such a family, nor had anyone else. In the sequel *Fripsey Summer* she shared the fun with this crazy family. Boys and girls love the things that go on. Ages 9-12.

That Wonderful Flight to the Mushroom Planet. Eleanor Cameron. Little. A story of two California boys who build a space ship and take off to visit a new planet, one peopled with odd-looking green creatures. Their adventures there makes one of the best space stories yet for the 9-12s.

Caddie Woodlawn. Carol Ryrie Brink. Illustrated by Kate Seredy. Macmillan. A Wisconsin frontier story laid about 1864. Caddie was a tomboy when girls were supposed to be ladies. A redhead, at eleven years old she was as strong and brown as a boy. With her two brothers she managed to get into a lot of trouble. The practical jokes they played on her Boston cousin brought disgrace. In spite of the mischief, Caddie was a warm, loving girl and once prevented a war between the Indians and the white men. Both boys and girls love this book, a series of adventures and fun. Other books by same author: *Magical Melons, All Over Town, Grandstand Family* (Viking).

The Bounces of Cynthiann. Evelyn S. Lampman. Illustrated by Grace Paull. Doubleday. Matthew, Marcia, Luke and Joanna, the four Bounces who came all the way from Rhode Island to live with their Uncle Seth after their parents died, take over the whole town of Cynthianna, Oregon. A wonderful picture of a pioneer town full of friendly people. Ages 8-12.

Ojibway Drums. Marian Magoon. Longmans. An interesting Indian story set in Canada. It is the story of a Chief's son who helps rescue his tribe from an enemy. There is lovely family feeling, humor and a great deal about the Ojibway customs. Ages 8-12.

Snow Treasure. Marie McSwigan. Dutton. Based on an actual happening in Norway, in the early days of the Nazi occupation. How a group of Norwegian children managed to get blocks of gold out of Norway by fastening them to their sleds and coasting through the German camp. Ages 9-12.

Train for Tiger Lily. Louise Riley. Viking. It was a very special kind of train that stopped one morning with its five young passengers at a place called Tiger Lily. Gus, the porter, was a magician, second class, who could do many mysterious things. There was a great deal of magic at work around the train. The children had lots of fun and excitement. This is one of the few books with a mixture of reality and magic that "clicks." Children like it. Ages 10-14.

Back to Treasure Island. Harold A. Calahan. Vanguard. Many people do not know of this continuation of Stevenson's *Treasure Island,* told in a style very like his. Beginning with characters in Stevenson's book and continuing situations which he had suggested, this is a dandy pirate and treasure story which any man or boy who read *Treasure Island* will enjoy. Ages 10-14.

Three Without Fear. Robert C. DuSoc. Longmans. Dave Rogers was shipwrecked off the coast of Baja, Lower California. He drifted ashore and joined two Indian children who were traveling on foot to find their grandmother. They had a perilous Robinson Crusoe sort of journey, and finally arrived where their families were. Boys especially are crazy about this book and like to own it. Ages 10-14.

Thad Owen. Hazel Wilson. Abingdon. Twelve-year-old Thad is the hero of this story. When he accidentally killed a neighbor's cow, trouble began for him. It was not until he confessed to his parents and "worked out" the price of the cow that things were better. Thad is a *real* boy and the Owen family is a *real* family. That, coupled with a good plot, makes a very readable book for both boys and girls. Ages 9-12. Another book by the same author: *The Owen Boys.*

Who Rides in the Dark? Stephen Meader. Harcourt. To consider just one title of this prolific and very excellent author's books would not be fair, and yet, to consider each would take too much space and time. As an author popular with both boys and girls, but especially boys (and boys from ten years old up to high school), he has written no "duds." That is to say, the children begin with one title and go right through everything he has written. And he has written about a great variety of subjects, from dogs and horses, to historic stories both on land and sea. This particular story concerns a fifteen-year-old boy who has a way with horses, gets a job helping in the stable at an inn in the early nineteenth century. There are mysterious doings that turn out to be caused by a band of rustlers. There is a fine atmosphere of the period plus an excellent story. As twelve-year-old Alex said, "He begins right away with action." Other titles: *Boy with a Pack, Clear for Action, King of the Hills, River of Wolves.* Any book of Meader's is a good story. In fact, the children just say "Give me another Meader." Ages 9-14.

Falcons of France. A tale of youth and the air. Charles Nordhoff and James N. Hall. Little. An incomparable story of an American boy in the Lafayette Flying Corps during the First World War. The authors themselves lived through many of the experiences they tell about. A moving story for adults as well as boys. Ages 12-20. Other famous stories by these famous authors: *Pearl Lagoon, The Derelict, Mutiny on the Bounty,* etc.

The Mutineers. Charles Hawes. Little. A tale of the old days at sea. Benjamin Lathrop, a sixteen-year-old, put out from Salem Harbor, a green hand on a sailing ship bound for China with a cargo of ginseng, and in the hold a fortune in gold. Murder and mutiny make this an appalling trip during which Benjamin played a man's part. An absorbing story and a "classic." The author is one of the best writers of the sea. It is sad that he died before he could do more than three books. Others are: *The Great Quest* and *Dark Frigate.* Ages 10-18.

Winter Danger. William O. Steele. Harcourt. A fairly new author in the juvenile field, and one of great promise. This particular book is the story of an eleven-year-old boy's efforts to adjust to the Tennessee Frontier village after life in the woods with his father. The people in this story are so fine, and the members of the family love each other. Other books by this good writer: *Buffalo Knife, Golden Roots, Over Mountain Boy, Tomahawks and Trouble.* Ages 8-12.

Wild Trek. Jim Kjelgaard (pronounced kyellgard). Holiday House. Kjelgaard is one of the most popular authors today, and this is one of his most popular books. I have had the exciting experience of reading this particular story aloud several times. It is wonderful to watch the appreciation of the children for the author's fine writing and the working out of the plot, and his knowledge of woodcraft. A trapper took with him only his gun, some supplies, and his dog, Chiri, and went to rescue two men who came down on the unexplored Caribou Mountains in the Canadian wilderness. It became a regular Robinson Crusoe story when one of the men went berserk, stole the supplies, gun, and even their boats, and left them stranded with no fire . . . nothing. How the two men got through, got fire from a burning tree, let Chiri kill their meat for them, and finally got out of the wilderness is a realistic, believable, exciting tale. The reader learns so much, too, about living in the wilds, without feeling that he is being instructed. This author has written many good books, all popular, on a great variety of subjects, from dog stories to historic fiction, wild-animal stories, and even one cave-man story. Some of the titles are: *Forest Patrol, A Nose for Trouble, Snow Dog, Chip the Dam Builder, Fire Hunter, Lion Hound.* Anything he has written is worthy as a gift for a youngster 10-16.

The Lion's Paw. Robb White. Doubleday. Many children would vote this their favorite book. Two orphans ran away from an asylum and joined a boy who was running away from an aunt and uncle because they were going to sell his boat. The boy's father had been reported missing during the war but the boy never gave up hope. His father had said he would see him when the boy found the lion's paw.

The three children have many exciting adventures and the end is a happy one. This author seems to get better all the time. Another popular title is *Candy,* a book girls of twelve and up are especially fond of—a modern story in which there is sailing and a slight mystery.

Jim Davis. John Masefield. McKay. A very interesting story of the Devonshire coast and smugglers a hundred years ago. Jim was captured by the smugglers. Ages 12-16. A classic.

Two Logs Crossing. Walter Edmonds. Dodd. A corking story for the twelve-year-old and up. Short, taking not more than an hour to read, it is based on a true incident in upper New York State at the beginning of the nineteenth century. It is a particularly moving story of a boy who trapped, suffered bad luck, and tried again, to pay a debt he thought his father had left. Good to read to a group. Another book by the same author appreciated by youngsters: *Tom Whipple.* Ages 12-16.

Pirates, Pirates, Pirates. Selected by Phyllis Fenner. Watts. Short stories taken from good books and magazines, designed to interest the boys and girls of Junior High age. Ages 10-16. Other collections by same author: *Speed, Speed, Speed, Fun, Fun, Fun, Heroes, Heroes, Heroes* (Watts), *Yankee Doodle, Circus Parade, Stories of the Sea* (Knopf).

Not all children like mysteries, but most do. And, as said, before, a good mystery is just as good for a child as any other kind of adventure. There is nothing wrong or strange in a child liking his stories to be "suspenseful." Here are some of the best-liked mysteries.

The Mystery of the Secret Drawer. Helen Fuller Orton. Lippincott. This is one of the many mysteries Mrs. Orton wrote for the young children. They are all mysteries of families, country, and village. Her "crimes" are about family money lost and found, a rare volume that turns up missing, lost stamps, a missing letter, noises in the chimney, caves. They are mysteries that the children of nine and ten who read them might solve themselves. They are extremely useful in encouraging children to read and to give them reading practice. The interesting thing is that the children read them several times. If you wish to buy books for your nine-year-old who isn't particularly fond of reading, or if he likes mysteries particularly, these are your books: *The Secret of the Pirate Oak, The Mystery of the Lost Letter, the Mystery in the Apple Orchard, The Mystery of the Old Cave, The Mystery of the Little Red School House,* and others. Ages. 8-10.

Five Bright Keys. Mary Urmston. Doubleday. A family moves into a new house that has, mysteriously, five keys. An everyday mystery story appreciated by ten-year-olds. Ages 9-12.

Pony Jungle. Lavinia Davis. Doubleday. "The jungle" was in a fashionable section of Connecticut and was patterned after a hobo jungle. There is a lot about horses in the story and a slight mystery. Ages 10-12. Other mysteries by same author: *The Plow Penny Mystery, Fishhook Island Mystery* (written under name of Wendel Farmer), *Donkey Detectives.* All of Mrs. Davis' books are excellent for children, and well liked by them.

The Dugout Mystery. Mary Graham Bonner. Knopf. In which you get not only baseball but a baffling mystery. Easy to read, and good for the young reader of nine and ten. Other titles by the same author: *The Haunted Hut, The Hidden Village Mystery, The Mysterious Caboose.* Ages 8-10.

The Cub Scout Mystery. Dorothy Sterling. Doubleday. A very good story of cub scouts who divide up the activities of a town to learn about their local affairs. One group getting the newspaper are disappointed because it sounds dull. To their surprise, it turns out to be the most exciting adventure when they turn up an old news item about a local crime. Boys ten to twelve will love it. I do too.

The Stranger in Primrose Lane. Noel Streatfeild. Randon House. A spy story of the last war in England in which some children of different ages, and from different families, through their own particular characteristics and abilities, catch a spy. The whole thing is so real. Parents will love reading it aloud. Ages 10-16. Another mystery by the same author: *The Secret of the Lodge.*

The Wabash Knows a Secret. Elizabeth Friermood. Doubleday. Illustrated by Grace Paull. A good family mystery taking place in the 1890's, and the solving of the great grandfather's murder and recovery of the wheat money that had been lost. It is a beautiful family, and a very good story. Interesting to twelve and up, especially girls.

The Island of the Dark Woods. Phyllis Whitney. Westminster. A Staten Island story, having to do with the legend of a ghostly stagecoach that traveled the old Richmond Turnpike on stormy nights. An old dark house, a lonely boy living with a crochety grandfather, a lost letter, a diary, two old coins, and two lively girls make a good mystery for the eleven- to fourteen-year-olds. Other mysteries by the same author: *The Mystery of the Gulls, The Black Diamond Mystery, The Mystery on the Isle of Skye.* Ages 10-14.

The Dagger, The Fish and Casey McKee. Electra Clark. McKay. One of the funniest and at the same time most exciting mysteries for youngsters I have read. A "character," Casey, comes to visit his queer uncle and runs into a full-blown mystery. Eventually Casey brings the gang of smugglers to justice. The humor is in the crazy characters making up the story and in the strange situations in which they often find themselves. You'll laugh, too, if you read it. Ages 10 and up.

Missing Brother. Keith Robertson. Viking. This author is worth investigating for your children's reading. A search for red clay and Indian arrowheads turns into an absorbing mystery involving money, gunplay and a long-missing brother. The hero is a real boy, and the action is fast. Others by the same author: *The Mystery of Burnt Hill, Three Stuffed Owls.* Ages 12-16.

The Captain's House. Elisabeth Kyle. Houghton. Folks in a tiny Scottish village think the English newcomers daft to rent the Captain's House. It had been deserted for years except for a wee bairn's ghost that haunts it. Fourteen-year-old Mollie helps the new family overcome a real danger and finally solve the secret of the haunted house. An excellent story from all angles. Ages 12-16.

The Captain's Secret. Harriet Weed Hubbell. Westminster. A mystery especially popular with girls. A girl was disappointed not to go on the sailing vessel with her father but finds plenty of excitement at home when a boy cousin comes to visit, and strange things happen. Cape Code in 1820. Ages 10-15.

The Tattooed Man. Howard Pease. Doubleday. A master of modern sea stories, this author has written a number of books about the ship *Araby* and its strong skipper, Captain Jarvis, and Tod Moran who ships with him. The author knows his sea, his ships, and his audience. In this particular story Tod Moran ships as an oil wiper. There is something mysterious about the *Araby* and very exciting things happen. Other titles: *The Jinx Ship, Secret Cargo, The Ship Without a Crew,* and others. Ages 10-16.

The Boys' Sherlock Holmes: A selection of the works of A. Conan Doyle. Howard Haycraft. Harper. Contains the stories that seem most appropriate for children. "Sign of the Four," "A Study in Scarlet," "The Speckled Band," etc. A good introduction to the great detective. Boys and girls ten and up.

The Father Brown Omnibus. G. K. Chesterton. Dodd. A little rosy cheeked, blue-eyed priest solves these mysteries. A collection of short stories. Will be enjoyed by everyone who likes mysteries. Ages twelve years old and up.

The Adventures of Richard Hannay. John Buchan. Houghton. Wonderful stories of Richard Hannay, an Englishman who, with courage and ingenuity, finds out secrets for his government with the help of two friends of equal cleverness. There are three full-length novels in this volume: *The Thirty Nine Steps, Green Mantle,* and *Mr. Standfast.*

The Secret Garden. Frances Hodgson Burnett. Scribner. An old story but still going strong. Mary, a bad-tempered, spoiled girl, is sent to live on a huge estate where she discovers a secret garden, its master and a sick boy, Colin. Dickon, the son of the maid, and Mary, take Colin to the secret garden. They not only make it bloom again but they begin to bloom themselves. Children of both sexes and of all ages seem to love this story. Ages 10-14.

It would seem as if Westerns were not as popular as they were years ago. Perhaps they have more exciting competition. There have been some good ones.

Smoky, The Cowhorse. Written and illustrated by Will James. Scribner. The range and corral, the round-up and rodeo, as seen through the eyes of a mouse-colored cow pony. Told in the vernacular of the cowboy. Won the Newbery Medal. A "classic." Ages 10-16. Others by the same author: *Lone Cowboy* (the author's own story and one of his best), *Sun Up.*

Cowboy Boots. Shannon Garst. Abingdon. A very readable book in which a boy learns a great deal about cowboy life and finds out that it is rewarding to be called a *real* cowboy. Easy to read. Ages 9-12.

Ride, Cowboy, Ride. William Warren. McKay. Danny, for his twelfth birthday, was allowed to go out to his father's cattle ranch to help with the spring roundup. He had a very exciting time. Easy to read. Ages 9-12.

Riders of the Gabilans. Graham Dean. Viking. A true picture of cowboy life today including roundups, cattle rustlers, and riding the range. Ages 12-16.

Cowboys, Cowboys, Cowboys. Stories selected by Phyllis Fenner. Watts. A collection of Western stories from books and magazines. The value, aside from pure pleasure, in a collection of stories taken from books is that it will usually lead children to go back to the original to read the whole story. Ages 10-14.

Sheep Wagon Family. Myra Richardson. Dodd. Cora Bell

was tired of wandering. She longed for a real house to live in, friends and school. A lovely family story of sheepherders, their trials and vicissitudes among the cattle men. Adventure, fun and heartaches.

Cattle Dog. Montgomery Atwater. Random House. A sixteen-year-old boy and his cattle dog guard more than a thousand Herefords on summer range. Told in ranch language, a fast-moving, easy-to-read and exciting story. Ages 10-14. Other titles by same author: *Rustlers of High Range, Avalanche Patrol.*

Mystery of Crystal Canyon. Rutherford Montgomery. Winston. When a squatter disappears near Lazy Y Ranch in Colorado, Kenny and his twin sister Pat solve the mystery with the help of the squatter's collie dog. Plenty of action. Ages 12-14.

Wild Horse of Rain Rock. William M. Rush. Longmans. Dan Gorden, a misfit on ranch G-G, was teased and bullied by the hands and ignored by his uncle. It was a hard job to prove his worth, but Dan did it. Fine story. Ages 12-16.

There have been a number of good sports stories the past few years. One of the most popular authors of sport stories, probably, is John R. Tunis who wrote so many excellent and popular books about the Dodgers, and other teams.

The Kid from Tompkinsville. John R. Tunis. Harcourt. The story of a rookie who made good in the major leagues. The people are so real in Mr. Tunis' books, the tempo so rapid, it is for all the world like listening to a broadcast right from the field. Others about professional baseball are: *Rookie of the Year, World Series, Kid Comes Back, Keystone Kids, Highpockets; Yea Wildcats* (about basketball). Ages 10-16. *Buddy and the Old Pro,* a story of an elementary school baseball team. Ages 10-14.

Crack of the Bat. Stories selected by Phyllis Fenner. Knopf. A collection of baseball stories from books and magazines is a popular anthology. Ages 10-14.

Fielder from Nowhere. Jackson Scholz. Morrow. Ken, a hero unknown, gets on the team by his good playing. Finally, his past catches up with him and threatens to ruin him, but all turns out well. The plot is an unusually good one. There is humor and good baseball. A topnotch story. Ages 10-16. Other good stories by the same author: *Gridiron Challenge, Soldiers at Bat, Pigskin Warriors.*

Southpaw from San Francisco. Philip Harkins. Morrow. Larry had been a spoiled arrogant boy. He was an excellent athlete but his own nature constantly interfered until life and his friends taught him better. A fine book with all the excitement of the diamond. Other books by the same author: *Punt Formation, Son of the Coach, Lightning on Ice* (Hockey). Ages 10-16.

The Basestealers. Mary G. Bonner. Knopf. The story of a boy who joins his P.A.L. baseball team. Boys from eight to twelve will enjoy this, especially the younger ones. Other books by the same author: *The Dugout Mystery, Out to Win.* All for the younger group.

Historic stories were my favorites but there were not as many modern stories to take my interest. Most children today seem to me more interested in the world around them. Here are some historic stories that are so well written and interesting that children of today do love them, especially if they are read to them.

The Courage of Sarah Noble. Alice Dalgliesh. Scribner. This is a "big" story although not a big book. Sarah Noble, aged nine, went into the Connecticut wilderness to cook for her father when he went to make a home for his family. Her courage, because she was really afraid, her maturity, because she had to be grown up, and finally, when all danger was over and the family united, her relief to be a little girl again, is a wonderful story. Ages 8-12.

The Golden Horseshoe. Elizabeth Coatsworth. Macmillan. Tamar, whose mother was an Indian Princess, was looked down upon by her half-brother. They lived on a plantation in Colonial days. Tamar, disguised as an Indian guide, went with an expedition to explore the wilderness. How she won the admiration and also the esteem of her mother's people is a very exciting story for youngsters ten to twelve. Another by the same author, *Sword of the Wilderness,* is a story of the French and Indian Wars and an American boy captured and taken to Canada. Ages 12-16.

The Matchlock Gun. Walter Edmonds. Dodd. Exciting is just the word for this story. Ten-year-old Edward Alstyne, while his father was away, saved his mother's life by firing an old Spanish gun that he had succeeded in placing on the table and aiming out of the window. A good story to read aloud. Children from nine up to any age will like it. Another historic story by the same author is *Wilderness Clearing.*

Treasure in the Little Trunk. Helen Fuller Orton. Lippincott. A story of early pioneering days in 1823 when a family left Vermont to make a new home in western New York. The mystery concerning the beads that disappeared is known to the reader. A lovely story of the sacrifice of a little girl for her sick mother, very lifelike. Ages 9-12. Other historic stories by the same author: *The Gold Laced Coat* (adventures of a French boy during the French and Indian Wars). *Hoofbeats of Freedom* (Long Island and Washington during the American Revolution).

Journey Cake. Isabel McMeekin. Messner. In 1793 Gordon Shadrow left his family while he went to Kentucky to make a new home for them. The wife died leaving six children in care of Juba, a free colored woman. Juba led her charges on the long trek until they were reunited with their father. A wonderfully exciting family story. The sequel, *Juba's New Moon,* is just as good. Girls especially like this. Ages 11-14.

Green Cockade. Merritt Parmelee Allen. Longmans. Ethan Allen and his Green Mountain Boys figure in this story. The Battle of Ticonderoga takes place, and the hero, Hal Stonebridge, took part in it. One of the nicest things about Allen's stories is the humor he brings into his historic tales. Boys and girls from ten up will like this. Others they like are: *White Feather, Johnny Reb, The Flicker's Feather.*

Silent Scot. Constance Lindsay Skinner. Macmillan. A series of stories about Andy McPhail, quick with the rifle, during the American Revolution on the frontier. Andy, a scout, and his Indian friend, Runner-on-the-Wind, have some thrilling escapes and adventures. Other stories by the same author: *Andy Breaks Trail, Becky Landers, Frontier Scout, Debby Barnes, Trader.*

Johnny Tremain. Esther Forbes. Houghton. A young reader said he wished this book were two hundred pages longer. It is called a "novel for young and old," and was awarded the Newbery Medal. Johnny was an apprentice to a goldsmith in Boston during the exciting year of the Tea Party and Battle of Lexington. When Johnny had his hand injured he became a courier for the Committee of Public Safety, and through him and his travels we see Boston during that period. Ages 12-16.

Rebel Siege. Jim Kjelgaard. Holiday. A story of the wilderness fighting of the Revolution and of Kinross McKenzie of Carolina who set out to get back his rifle stolen by a British officer. He saw a great deal of fighting until the British surrendered at King's Mountain. A very superior story for boys and girls because it shows the reasons why the people fought. Ages 11-15.

Black Falcon. Story of piracy and old New Orleans. Armstrong Sperry. Winston. Wade Thayer and his negro servant are shipwrecked on the island where Jean Lafitte, known as the Black Falcon, has his camp. Wade sails with Lafitte in his privateering raids against the British. An exciting book full of pirates and battles at sea. One boy said, "I like it because it has such a variety of things happening." Ages 11-15. Another historic story by same author: *Storm Canvas.*

Deerslayer. James Fenimore Cooper. Scribner. A rousing

tale of warfare between the Iroquois Indians and the white settlers in the middle of the 18th century. The chief characters are Hawkeye, Uncas, and two sisters, Judith and Hetty. While the pace is slower than books written today, and there is a great deal of description, the boys especially still like it. There is a lovely illustrated edition of it in the Scribner's Classics Series, illustrated by N. C. Wyeth. *The Last of the Mohicans* is by the same author and comes in the same edition. Ages 12-16.

IX

"*Animals are such agreeable friends.*"

ANIMAL STORIES

ALMOST ALL CHILDREN, big and little, love stories about animals, wild and tame. Children seem to feel close to little animals. They anguish with them and rejoice when things turn out all right. Cruelty to animals they will not tolerate. They can take better man's cruelty to man. Stories of children and their pets, of faithful dogs, of clever, cute cats, of tame deer and raccoons, of monkeys and elephants, never seem to lose their popularity.

This list is a selection of some of the best known and most popular. There are only a few old stories, and they are the ones like *Black Beauty* that the children will not let go of.

Favorite Animal Books

Horse Stories

Twinkle, A Baby Colt. Lawrence Barrett. Knopf. A very sweet little colt that little children feel akin to. Ages 4-8.

Flip. Story and pictures by Wesley Dennie. Viking. Flip, the little colt, was afraid to jump the stream but after he had a dream that he had wings and flew over he did it without even thinking. Easy to read and beautiful. Ages 4-8.

Little Appaloosa. Written and illustrated by Berta and Elmer Hader. Macmillan. Ben's father gave him an Indian pony, a little appaloosa, for his birthday. Their merry adventures included helping to save the life of the chief of an Indian tribe. Ages 7-9.

Billy and Blaze. Written and illustrated by C. W. Anderson. Macmillan. Lovely picture book of Billy who loved horses, especially his pony Blaze, and of the adventures they had together. Also *Blaze and the Forest Fire, Blaze and the Gypsies, Blaze Finds the Trail,* and *Blaze and Thunderbolt.* Ages 6-8.

A Pony for Linda. Written and illustrated by C. W. Anderson. Macmillan. Linda was given Daisy, a pony, when she was seven. She rode in a horse show and made a friend. Ages 6-8. Sequel: *Linda and the Indians.*

The Little Wild Horse. Story and pictures by Hetty Burlingame Beatty. Houghton. How Peter longs for a horse, and how his wish comes true. Beautifully illustrated ranch story. Ages 6-7.

Star of Wild Horse Canyon. Clyde Bulla. Crowell. Wonderful because it is such a good story and so easy to read. Older boys who have trouble reading like this story. Ages 7-12.

Blue Canyon Horse. Ann Nolan Clark. Illustrations by Allen Mouser. Viking. A boy's love for his beautiful horse, his grief when she wanders away to join a wild herd, and his joy when she returns with her colt, are told in beautiful poetic words. The story is unusually good, as one would expect from this author, and the pictures are colorful and right. Ages 8-12.

A Pony Called Lightning. Miriam Mason. Illustrated by C. W. Anderson. Macmillan. The story of a Western pony whose ambition was to race with Lightning and to win. One day he did. Excellent for beginning readers. Ages 7-9.

Dynamite, the Wild Stallion. Nils Hogner. Aladdin Books. Shorty tamed the beautiful wild stallion by kindness and patience. Excellent for young readers who are having a little trouble. Ages 7-9.

Red Joker. Written and illustrated by Margaret Johnson.

Morrow. Red Joker, an Irish setter, helped train a promising colt and traveled with him to races all over the country. Ages 8-12.

Sleighbells for Windy Foot. Frances Frost. McGraw. Story of a New England Christmas and Toby and Windy Foot. Other stories about the same combination: *Windy Foot at the County Fair, Maple Sugar for Windy Foot.* Ages 8-12. All very popular with children.

Misty of Chincoteague. Marguerite Henry. Illustrated by Wesley Dennis. Rand. Two children get a pony from Assateague and Chincoteague Islands on pony-penning day. A beautiful book and beautiful story appreciated by children from 8 to 14. Other books by author: *King of the Wind, Brighty of Grand Canyon.*

Justin Morgan Had a Horse. Marguerite Henry. Illustrated by Wesley Dennis. Wilcox. Justin Morgan, a schoolteacher, took a little colt that no one else wanted. That colt grew to be the first in a long line of famous American horses. A magnificent story. As one girl wrote: "It is the most wonderful book of its kind. I think it will live forever. The story is very sad but has a wonderful ending." Ages 9-14.

Old Bones, The Wonder Horse. Mildred Pace. Illustrated by Wesley Dennis. McGraw. A homely horse with a big heart and almost human intelligence came out of nowhere to win the Kentucky Derby and run a hundred races before his retirement. Boys and girls love this story of a great heart. Ages 10-16.

A Horse to Remember. Genevieve T. Eames. Illustrated by Paul Brown. Messner. A boy overcomes his fear of riding through his friendship with a horse. Ages 9-14.

Black Stallion. Walter Farley. Random House. The popularity of this book has been phenomenal. A seventeen-year-old boy and a black stallion are the only survivors of a shipwreck. Back in the United States the boy and an old jockey train the wild horse for racing. Ages 10-16. Other titles about the boy and horse are: *Black Stallion Returns, Son of Black*

Stallion, Black Stallion and Satin, Blood Bay Colt, Black Stallion's Fury.

Horses, Horses, Horses. Stories selected by Phyllis Fenner. Illustrated by Pers Crowell. Watts. Seventeen horse stories from books and magazines. Ages 10-14.

Kentucky Derby Winner. Isabel McMeekin. McKay. A story of Aristides, the first horse to win the Kentucky Derby. Based on fact. A nice family story. Ages 9-12.

Red Horse Hill. Stephen Meader. Harcourt. After his father's death Bud found a home on a New Hampshire farm where he was given a colt to raise. His winning of the cutter race and finding an old will helped him to go to college. An excellent story, and probably the start to reading more books by this good author. Sequel: *Cedar's Boy,* a race-track story.

Silver Saddles. Covelle Newcomb. Longmans. A fifteen-year-old boy brings a valuable palomino to his father's ranch in Mexico through bandit-infested country. Ages 12-14.

Blind Colt. Written and illustrated by Glen Rounds. Holiday. Whitey finds a blind colt in a mustang band and trains it. A beautifully written story, unforgettable. Ages 10-14. By same author: *Stolen Pony.*

Black Beauty. Helen Sewell. In many editions. A horse tells his own story. I have left until last this most popular of all horse stories in spite of its age and sentimentality. The children of today, as the children of yesterday, just *love* it. Ages 8-12.

Books About Horses

Thoroughbreds. Written and illustrated by C. W. Anderson. Macmillan. How to judge a horse, illustrated with wonderful black-and-white lithographs of different kinds of horses. Stories of famous horses are woven into the text. Ages 12-14.

Heads Up, Heels Down. A handbook of horsemanship. Written and illustrated by C. W. Anderson. Macmillan. The most popular book on how to ride. Ages 10-14.

First Book of Horses. Isabel McMeekin. Pictures by Pers Crowell. Watts. Young readers are introduced to the different breeds of horses, their characteristics, their work, their care. Ages 8-12.

Horses and How to Draw Them. Amy Hogeboom. Vanguard. Different kinds of horses are pictured with directions for drawing them. Ages 8-12.

Dog Stories

Burlap. Written and illustrated by Morgan Dennis. Viking. Burlap was supposed to be a bunny chaser but he wouldn't. An amusing story that delights children. Ages 5-7.

Barney of the North. Written and illustrated by Margaret S. Johnson. Morrow. This author has written many good horse and dog stories for young children. In this story a Newfoundland puppy proves himself a hero after a train wreck. Ages 7-9. Other dog stories by this author: *Rolf, An Elkhound of Norway, Gay, A Shetland Sheep Dog, Lancelot and Scamp.*

Beanie. Written and illustrated by Ruth and Latrobe Carrol. Oxford. A picture-story book about a little six-year-old and his dog and what happened when he met a bear in the woods and lost his puppy. Sequel: *Tough Enough.* Very lovely family stories. Ages 6-8.

The Highly Trained Dogs of Professor Petit. Carol Ryrie Brink. Macmillan. Professor Petit and his trained dogs were down on their luck when they met Willie who found jobs for all of them. Children are crazy about this story. Ages 9-12.

Always Reddy. Marguerite Henry. Illustrated by Wesley Dennis. McGraw. A warm and lovely story of a thoroughbred Shamrock Queen (Irish setter) and what happened in the City Hall when she was thought to be past her usefulness as a hunter. Ages 8-12.

Ginger Pye. Eleanor Estes. Harcourt. Ginger was a puppy bought by young Jerry and Rachel Pye for a dollar. The Pye family was happy until a mysterious man appeared and Ginger disappeared. A nice family story. Ages 9-14.

Us and the Duchess. Edward Fenton. Doubleday. A story of Joel and his silver setter, the mysterious Duchess, and the heartache when he thought she was gun shy, and the rejoicing when she really became his. Ages 10-14.

Dogs, Dogs, Dogs. Stories selected by Phyllis Fenner. Illustrated by Manning DeV. Lee. Watts. A baker's dozen of dog stories from *The Call of the Wild, Bob, Son of Battle,* and other good books. Ages 10-14.

Big Red. Jim Kjelgaard. Holiday. Danny was given an Irish Setter to train. They roamed the wilderness, hunting, fishing, tracking bears. Both grew up in the process. An excellent story for anyone of any age. There is plenty of humor here too. Ages 10-16. Other dog books by the same author: *Irish Red, Outlaw Red, Snow Dog, Nose for Trouble.*

Lassie Come Home. Eric M. Knight. Illustrated by Marguerite Kirmse. Winston. This book got almost as many votes as *Black Beauty* for the favorite book of several hundred children. Young children as well as older children adore it. When Lassie was sold and taken to northern Scotland she made the four-hundred-mile trek back home. A terrific story. Ages 8-16. "I liked Lassie because the way the author wrote it, you seemed to be sharing all of the pain and happiness of the dog," wrote Gerald.

Silver Chief, Dog of the North. Jack O'Brien. Illustrated by Kurt Wiese. Winston. An adventure story of the Canadian Wilderness in which Silver Chief, son of a husky and a wolf, is the hero. He is trained by a Canadian Mounted Policeman, and together they have many exciting times. Sequel: *Return of Silver Chief* and *Silver Chief to the Rescue.* Both boys and girls love these stories for the adventures as well as the dog story. Ages 10-14.

Call of the Wild. Jack London. Illustrated by Paul Bransom. Macmillan. One of the greatest of dog stories and loved by children. A St. Bernard dog in the Klondike after mistreatment finally reverted and became the leader of a pack of wolves. Ages 10-16.

Hudson Bay Express. Robert Davis. Illustrated by Henry Pitz. Holiday. Two boys, one white and one Indian, live on the shore of James Bay in Canada. They train dogs and organize a dog-team freight-and-passenger line. An excellent story, and different. Ages 12-16.

Lad: A Dog. Albert Payson Terhune. Dutton. A biography of a collie. Very much loved. Other books by same author: *Bruce, Heart of a Dog.*

Dignity, A Springer Spaniel. Col. S. P. Meek. Knopf. Colonel Meek is one of the most popular authors of dog stories among the ten- to twelve-year-olds. There are better stories, perhaps, but none more popular. This particular one has to do with the loyalty between a man and his dog. Others by the same author: *Frantz, a Dog of the Police; Omar, a State Police Dog; Boy, an Ozark Coon Hound.*

Big Mutt. John H. Reese. Westminster. Big Mutt, abandoned on the highway in the Badlands, becomes a sheep killer. A boy, who believed in him saved him from being killed. As one young reader says: "From the moment you start reading *Big Mutt* you have a feeling of sympathy for the dog and his troubles."

Yipe. David Malcolmson. Illustrated by Morgan Dennis. Little. A moving story of a dog, cast off by its owners, who adopts a farm family. She devotes herself to protecting her mistress and helping her master. There is sadness in this story, too, and an understanding of both people and dogs. Ages 8-12.

Books About Dogs

American Champions. Text and pictures by Gladys Cook. Macmillan. Seventy-four breeds of dogs are described, each one identified by a black-and-white sketch of one of its famous champions. Brief descriptions, appearance, personality and size of each dog. Ages 8-14.

So You're Going to Get a Puppy. Colonel S. P. Meek. Knopf. A very practical guide to buying, owning and training a dog. Ages 10-14.

First Book of Dogs. Gladys Taber. Watts. Information about various breeds of dogs, their characteristics, care and training. Ages 7-9.

Dogs and How to Draw Them. Amy Hogeboom. Vanguard. Just what the title says it is. These books of how to draw animals are very popular with children. Ages 7-12.

Cat Stories

Lullaby. Josephine Bernhard. Illustrated by Irena Lorentowicz. Roy. A Christmas tale of the Christ Child and the little cat that sings Him to sleep. Ages 5-8.

Green Eyes. Story and pictures by Abe Birnbaum. Capitol. The high spots in the first year of a cat's life. Told in first person. Ages 5-7.

Fishing Cat. Grayce Silverton Myers. Illustrated by Paul Galdone. Abingdon. Skipper helped his master fish, and when Old John hurt his arm Skipper did all the work. Ages 5-7.

April's Kittens. Written and illustrated by Claire Newberry. Harper. When April's cat Sheba had three kittens it became a problem in their "one-cat apartment" until Father solved the problem. Ages 5-7.

Fish Head. Jean Fritz. Coward. A rollicking story of a rapscallion cat, Fish Head, who inadvertently took a voyage that proved to be pleasanter than his life on the waterfront had been. A real character is Fish Head. Ages 7-9.

Joey and Patches. Written and illustrated by Margaret Johnson. Morrow. The story of two six-weeks-old kittens as they emerge with entirely different characteristics which lead them into different kinds of adventures. Ages 6-8.

Tippy. Sally Scott. Illustrated by Beth Krush. Harcourt. When Tippy's brothers and sisters had all gone off he set out to find a new home where he could have company. Ages 6-8.

Fancy be Good. Written and illustrated by Audrey Chalmers. Viking. The tale of twin kittens, one who was good and one who was bad. A charming book with delightful pictures. Ages 6-9. Another by the same author: *Kitten's Tale.* Ages 5-7.

The Cat That Went to College. Frances Frost. Illustrated by Wesley Dennis. McGraw. A stray kitten was taken in by a college boy where it made its home for the rest of the year, attending classes and receiving a report card at the end. Children love it. Beautiful pictures. Ages 8-12.

Elijah the Fishbite. Agnes Turnbull. Macmillan. The minister's children named the stray cat that adopted them that dignified name because it appeared on the morning their father preached about Elijah. The children got into difficulties because of the kitten but Elijah saved the situation once or twice, too. One of the nicest cat stories I know. Ages 8-12.

Lucky Blacky. Eunice Lackey. Watts. A very popular book partly because it is about an amusing cat and an amusing old woman, but also because it is so easy to read. Children who are just beginning can read it to themselves. Ages 6-9.

Mère Michel and Her Cat. Retold by Margaret Cardew. Illustrated with some of the drawings that appeared in the original edition. Day. Had the cat not had nine lives he would never have lasted until the end of the story. He was a tough cat in Paris during the eighteenth century and he fought his way from one blood curdling escapade to another with an archenemy after him all the time. Ages 8-12. Children love this read aloud, and the older person reading it enjoys it just as much.

Books About Cats

Cats. Written and illustrated by Wilfrid Bronson. Harcourt. All kinds of cats are in this book for young children, with their physical characteristics, instincts and habits described. Ages 7-12.

First Book of Cats. Gladys Taber. Watts. Includes information about various breeds of cats, how to take care of them, what they should have to eat, etc. Excellent. Ages 7-9.

All Kinds of Cats. Walter Chandoha. Photographs by author. Knopf. Over one hundred photographs of cats with brief text. All ages.

Cats and How to Draw Them. Amy Hogeboom. Vanguard. For the children who like to draw, these are simple suggestions. Very popular with little children. Ages 7-10.

Other Pet Stories

Show Lamb. Hildreth Wriston. Abingdon. An affectionate story of a Vermont family on a sheep farm with Chad, the nine-year-old hero. Chad's father couldn't understand why he wanted a lamb of his own, so Chad secretly picked one. He picked a good one too. Lots of adventure and family fun. Ages 8-12.

Pete the Parrakeet. Irma S. Black. Holiday. An easy-to-read story of a pet that is becoming more and more popular today. Pete's amusing tricks lead him from one master to another until he finally finds Andy who understands and loves him. Ages 8-10.

Wild Animal Adventure

Here Come the Bears. Alice Goudey. Scribner. True life stories about American bears: grizzly, polar, Alaskan brown-and-black. Simply told. Delightful illustrations. Children love it. By the same author: *Here Come the Deer.* Equally popular. Ages 6-9.

Slim Green. Louise D. Harris and Norman D. Harris. Little. The story of a little green snake that pleases small children very much. Ages 6-9.

Bambi. Felix Salten. Many editions. The life story of a deer poetically told. A classic that all children love. Ages 8-12.

Rufous Redtail. Helen Garrett. Viking. Rufous is a hawk and this is his life story from the time he hatches until he takes a mate and raises a family. Humor and vitality in this story. Boys especially love it. Ages 10-14.

Kildee House. Rutherford G. Montgomery. Illustrated by Barbara Cooney. Doubleday. This is an author to remember when you want to buy a book for your ten- to twelve-, or older, year-old boy who is crazy about wild animals. This is an amusing story of a shy man who wanted seclusion and built himself a house under a giant redwood tree. He didn't mind one skunk family or one raccoon but when they began to multiply it was different. I remember a boy telling his class about this story—he laughed so he could hardly go on with his tale. Ages 10-14. *Carcajou* by the same author.

The Jungle Book. Rudyard Kipling. Doubleday. This should not be forgotten when thinking of animal stories. Children love it, especially read aloud. Don't forget that it includes not only the Mowgli stories but those two stories incomparable and absolutely necessary to a child, *Rikki Tikki Tavi* and *Toomai of the Elephants.* Ages 10-14.

Mojave Joe. Dustin C. Scott. Knopf. A moving story of a famous Western coyote who yearned to be near man, how he was captured, taken to a zoo, escaped and returned home hundreds of miles away. As appealing as a dog story. Ages 10-14.

Lions on the Hunt. Theodore Waldeck. Illustrated by Kurt Wiese. Viking. Written by a master of wild-animal stories extremely popular with both boys and girls. This particular story is about Sur-Dah, a young African lion who grew up to be chief of his pack. As one young reader wrote: "It is the most exciting book I have ever read. It is one of the few books that started out real exciting . . . the book report may not raise your interest, but I'm sure you will love the book." Ages 10-14. Other books by same author, equally exciting: *Jamba the Elephant, The White Panther, Treks Across the Veldt, On Safari.*

Books About Wild Life

Big Zoo. William Bridges. Photographs by Desider Holisher. Viking. The story of a zoo, the animals who live there and the people who take care of them. Ages 9-12. Other books by the same author: *True Zoo Stories,* Ages 7-10; *Zoo Babies,* Ages 6-8.

Desert Animals. Rita Kissin. Illustrated by Helen Carter. McKay. Little-known desert animals described in rhymed text with colored pictures. Very popular with little children. Ages 5-8.

Horns and Antlers. Written and illustrated by Wilfrid Bronson. Harcourt. All about the deer and antelopes of North America in detailed picture story. This author writes in such a readable, slightly humorous style that children love his books. Ages 8-14. Other books by same author: *The Chiseltooth Tribe* (little animals); *The Grasshopper Book* (insects); *Wonderworld of Ants.*

X

"The excitement is mentel."

QUIET STORIES

"THESE STORIES don't have action like shooting someone," wrote the boy about *The Puppet Man.* "The excitement is mentel."

Isn't it strange how difficult it is for us grownups to put ourselves back into childhood and remember what we liked? With what trepidation and self-consciousness I, for instance, read a quiet story to children for a first time! Wouldn't you think I'd remember, not only some of my own childhood favorites, but also experiences I have had with children? Children, contrary to the belief of many grownups, love quiet stories in certain moods, just as we do.

I had a manuscript sent to me to try with the children. It was *The Puppet Man,* by Barbara Young, a collection of little stories by a poet . . . quiet little stories with imagination, humor, and a touch of magic, the kind that children take to their hearts and hold forever. The children adored it, boys and girls alike. Quick to sense genuine feeling, their comments were not only from their hearts but were expressed poetically, "like an unrhymed poem"; "It was so real and had a lot of feeling"; "It is like hills, short hills. You have to come down one to go up another or you would walk in circles." "They were nice, like going to bed."

I suppose the answer to all this is how well the book is written. If a story doesn't have action to sustain it, the writing must be so good, the feeling of the author so genuine, that the story is convincing.

Goodnight Moon and *The Goodnight Book,* both by Margaret Wise Brown are examples of quiet books that children like. Alvin Tresselt's *White Snow, Bright Snow; Hi, Mr. Robin,* are others that satisfy children's inner something.

When I read *Pinky Finds a Home* the children's comments proved how much they loved this quiet little book. "It couldn't be all exciting. You wouldn't get a chance to rest if it was all exciting."

Favorite "Quiet" Stories

Many Moons. James Thurber. Illustrated by Louis Slobodkin. Harcourt. A quiet story with quiet humor. The little princess wants the moon. No one can suggest how to get it. The jester goes to see the little princess to ask her where it is, and how big it is. It is not very far away, she says because it is often caught in the branches outside her window. And it is slightly smaller than her thumb nail because when she holds her thumb up she can cover it. So the jester has a gold moon made for her and she is happy. The charm of this story can be felt best when it is read aloud to children.

The Street of Little Shops. Margery Bianco. Doubleday. One of my favorite books, and I am pleased to say, popular with little and big children. It is a collection of little stories without much plot, having to do with shops in a little town: "Mr. A. and Mr. P.," "Mr. Murdle's Large Heart," "Hats for Horses," and so on. Read it to the children and they want to read it themselves right away. A twelve-year-old youngster told me she always read it when she was sick in bed. Children in the third grade can read it easily themselves, and yet, there is no top limit on the age of enjoyment. Parents love it. A book for all people, and a quiet book.

Ragman of Paris. Elizabeth Orton Jones. Oxford. Another example of quiet stories pleasing to children. Mich and Tobie are picked up by the Ragman for a bundle of rags. He takes them home where Madame Pouf makes them new shirts out of her numerous petticoats. The boys have many quiet adventures with the Ragman. Ages 4-6.

Peter Plants a Pocketful. Aaron Fine. Oxford. A story for the youngest. Peter planted a seed and forgot it. Later it became a wonderful flower. A colorful picture book. Ages 3-6.

This Boy Cody. Leon Wilson. Watts. A Tennessee mountain story. Ten-year-old Cody has quiet adventures with his family, going bee tracing, a housewarming, a day with riddles. Quiet family life and everyday happenings, but so well told they gleam unusually bright. Ages 8-12. Sequel: *This Boy Cody and His Friends*.

The Poppy Seeds. Clyde Bulla. Crowell. One of the loveliest of the new books for little children is this story of Pablo who, with his poppy seeds, brought not only water and flowers but good will to the people of his dusty valley. Ages 5-8.

Rabbit Hill. Written and illustrated by Robert Lawson. Little. One of the loveliest stories and most beautiful books to look at, about the little animals on Rabbit Hill, who got to know and love the new family that moved in; and in the sequel, *Tough Winter,* have a hard winter when the family leaves the place in the hands of a bad caretaker with a dog. Children adore these stories. Absolute necessities in a child's life. Preferably read them aloud. Good for all ages.

The Blue Cat of Castletown. Catherine Cate Coblentz. Longmans. A quiet story with real magic is this tale of the blue cat in a Vermont town who seeks out a friendly hearth and brings the owner the beauty and wisdom of the river's song. Ages 8-12.

Miss Hickory. Carolyn Sherwin Bailey. Viking. The quiet happenings in a barnyard when a doll with an hickory-nut head and an apple-tree twig for a body is left to struggle in a New Hampshire winter. Needs to be read to children. Ages 6-12.

Mr. Tidy Paws. Frances Clark Sayers. Viking. When Christopher went to earn money for his grandmother, the black cat, Mr. Tidy Paws, went with him. They joined a dog-and-pony circus and Mr. Tidy Paws was such a wonderful performer Christopher went home with lots of money. Ages 8-12.

Mountain Born and *Once in a Year.* Elizabeth Yates. Coward.Two charming stories by a master of the beautiful quiet story. In the first, a little boy and his pet lamb help a wise old shepherd and his dog care for a whole flock of sheep. In the second, using the same characters, the author retells two old Christmas legends of the flowering forest and of the animals talking at midnight. Ages 8-12.

Paddle to the Sea. Written and illustrated by Holling C. Holling. Houghton. A toy canoe with a seated Indian figure was launched by an Indian boy who had carved it. In four years it traveled through all the Great Lakes and the St. Lawrence River to the Atlantic. *Seabird* and *Tree in the Trail* are two others by this same author. Ages 8-12.

That Boy Johnny. Evelyn R. Sickels. Scribner. A New England story in the 1870's, each chapter a little story about Johnny, but all tied together with the episode in the first story when Johnny's first pair of trousers blew away, and ending when they are recovered months later. Ages 6-8.

The Cat Who Went to Heaven. Elizabeth Coatsworth. Macmillan. A three-colored cat brought good luck to a Japanese artist who was working on a picture for the temple, introducing animals one after another. A beautiful story, not very long. Ages 8-12.

Benjamin West and His Cat Grimalkin. Marguerite Henry. Bobbs. Benjamin was a Quaker boy who lived in Pennsylvania when it belonged to England. His family disapproved of his making pictures but at the suggestion of his cat, who could almost talk, Benjamin practiced and became a great painter. The story of Benjamin West will be appreciated especially by children interested in drawing, and also by cat lovers. Ages 8-12.

The Moffats. Eleanor Estes. Harcourt. There are four young Moffats who lived with their mother in Connecticut. They may be poor in worldly goods but not in things of the spirit. The story is told through Jane who is nine. The popularity of this book, and of the other Moffat stories, has earmarked it for the classic class already. The activities of the family are quiet and everyday, and seem to be very satisfactory to all children. Sequels: *The Middle Moffat, Rufus M.* Ages 10-14.

Li Lun, Lad of Courage. Carolyn Treffinger. Abingdon. A Chinese boy who was afraid of the sea and would not go on his first fishing voyage was sent to plant rice on the mountain. His courage and patience in the face of what seems impossible is a wonderful story for children. Ages 10-14.

Maggie Rose: Her Birthday Christmas. Ruth Sawyer. Harper. A little Maine girl sells berries so that her shiftless family may celebrate a wonderful birthday Christmas and repay the neighbors for their many kindnesses. It is a charming story of a real little personality, and of a family who, though shiftless, are also charming. This story will be enjoyed by the whole family at Christmas, or at any time during the year. Ages 8-14.

One-String Fiddle. Erick Berry. Winston. A mountain boy, in order to get a collar for his beloved dog, enters a fiddling contest. He makes up his tune from the everyday noises he hears. An unusual story, full of humor and charm. Ages 8-12.

Fog Magic. Julia Sauer. Viking. Greta, who always loved the fog, was one day in it when she found a secret village. It is a perfect combination of fantasy (a child's own little magic world) and realism, with a love of the woods and sea.

Girls love this particularly well. As one child said: "It makes such pretty pictures in my head." Ages 10-14.

Tall Hunter. Howard Fast. Harper. Richard Hammond, a wanderer, finally married Ellen May and settled down. One day he wandered off and when he returned his home was gone and Ellen May a captive of the Indians. Johnny Appleseed helped him find them. A beautifully told story, good for family reading. Very poetic in quality. Kentucky frontier. Ages 12 and up.

Saint Santa Claus. Ruth Rounds. Dutton. A modern story beginning with a plane crash in the Swiss Alps in which the only survivors were a little boy and a smaller girl. How they were helped to the village by a monk who had lived five hundred years before sounds fantastic, but the author has made this miracle so real that children adore that part best of all. A Christmas story. Ages 10-14.

I have left until last my own favorite quiet books:

Roller Skates. Ruth Sawyer. Viking (Newberry Medal book). For one never-to-be-forgotten year Lucinda lived in New York, away from her strict parents. She roller skated every place. It was in the 1890's. She made many friends, from Mr. Gilligan, the hack driver, to Tony, son of the fruit vendor. It has sadness as well as humor. Lucinda's escapades are something and, with it all, her enchanting personality and gaity permeate the book. It is based on a true year in the author's life. Not every child will enjoy this, but I have known many children to love it best of all. Grownups adore it. Ages 12 and up.

The Wind in the Willows. Kenneth Grahame. Illustrated by Ernest Shepard. Scribner. (There are other editions with different illustrators. This is my favorite.) The incomparable tale of Water Rat, Mole, Toad, Badger and other animals who live on the river and in the woods. You will find all of the characters so real they are like people to you. The language is so beautiful, the wisdom so kindly, the humor so gentle, that the book can be read and reread forever. I have heard that the author modeled his characters after friends of his. The adventures of the vain Mr. Toad are hilariously funny. The quiet adventures of the water rat and the mole are more satisfying.

I had asked Alex, a twelve-year-old boy who read everything, to read it. He didn't return it for a long time, so that I thought he probably didn't like it. One morning, and it was a morning when I needed encouragement, Alex returned the book. He settled down beside my desk and said, "Was it *mel*-LOW, oh boy!" I said, "You really liked it?" "Oh, yes," he answered, "Do you know why? It was such a cozy book."

These books I have just been telling you about are all "cozy" books, good for all time.

XI

"Only one bad spot."

FOR LADIES ONLY

"My mother wants to know if you think I'd like *Drums Along the Mowhawk,*" asked Dick, as he stood beside my desk. He was referring to the movie. "I don't know," I said doubtfully (he was only nine). "It's a love story." "Well," he said, screwing his face all up, "we saw a preview. There wasn't much love in it. Only one bad spot." Boys don't care much for love.

In the very beginning, in the picture-book stage, boys and girls don't seem so different in their choice of books—except, of course, for little boys' love of mechanical things which most girls do not share. But at the time when they are just beginning to read for themselves boys and girls go in different directions. Girls will read most of the books boys read plus the little-girl stories and some other special things. I doubt if you ever find a boy who has read a love story until he is in high school and reading adult novels. Boys seldom read horse stories either, even if they are about boys. The demand is from the girls.

When girls begin to read for themselves they love stories about pets, and families, and little girls. They love fairy tales, the romantic-princess sort of story. They love stories about adopted children, of stepchildren, of problem children.

Sentimental stories they like to weep over. Then comes the time, at twelve or so, when they ask of a book, in a whisper, "Is there any love in it?" By the next year they are openly demanding love in big letters. The stories they consider love stories would scarcely be recognized by an adult as romance. There is usually only a suggestion. No love scenes. Teen-age books, so-called even by the girls themselves, or Junior novels, a more dignified title, are often marked *High School Age* or 14-16. These books are usually read by the children from eleven and twelve (sixth grade) and on up, until during freshman year in high school they read the adult books.

Most of these teen-age books are not great literature. Some of them may be long lived. They do fill a great need because girls at that age need something for their emotions, their questions, for their growing up. And they also need them as a preparation for the sophisticated adult novel that is rampant nowadays. The more background they have of the good solid literature when they are little, and of the books for their own particular age as they are adolescent, the better they will be able to "take" the modern novel, the more perspective they will have for it. I remember a boy in high school who was asked to read *Winesburg, Ohio,* by Sherwood Anderson. He was a boy who had not been a great reader. He was quite visibly shocked by the stories. He said, "I guess they want us to grow up fast." Had he had more background of reading it would have been different.

The books for girls are comparatively recent. I once sat next to an elderly woman in a class at Columbia. She told me of the advent of *Little Women,* how excited she was when she saw it. She ran all the way home. It was the first book for girls in which girls were human, real, and in which the story had any "umph" at all. Girls' books had been pretty sappy up to that time. And it really is only within the last ten years that there have been good girls' books in any quantity.

Girls are interested in *career* books. They are a product of these times. You'll find a book about almost every known career for girls. There is a big market for them because girls like them, and because they are about career people, so purchasers think they must be worth while. The trouble is, with most of them, the career is not really important to the girls. It is the story the career hangs on that they like. And it does not show that girls are interested in any particular career that they read these books. For the most part they are not particularly good. Once in a while there happens to be a book that is excellent that does involve some kind of career. *Middle Button,* for example, is about a girl who studies medicine. The author of it was thinking more of her people and her story than of the career. Then you have something. But the endless series about nurses, interior decorators, artists, and so on, are just like any series books, they are feeble and thin. Girls do like them, though.

A word about Nancy Drew. If you have not heard about her in your home, then doubtless you do not have a girl in the family. Another name for books about her is "Caroline Keene mysteries," Caroline Keene being her creator. These are cheap run-of-the-mill thrillers in which Nancy Drew performs all kinds of stunts, solves mysteries involving high-powered motor cars and expensive perfumes. Girls like them. And if they are going through the throes of Nancy Drew you can't argue. *They like them.* Someone told me once that if Nancy Drew were to be read aloud to an admirer, it would all sound so ridiculous the fanatical reader would be cured for ever. I never tried it, but it might be worth a try. The trouble is, if enough Nancy Drews and such are read by a youngster, she has no perspective for anything else. They are unreal, impossible, and the plots are a dime a dozen. There are counterparts among the boys' books, various series that are turned out by a factory someplace. The thing parents can do is to provide better fare along with Nancy so that Nancy is not the only reading the girls have. You can't tell them why they are bad. *But you don't have to buy them for your daughters.* I suspect most of the Caroline Keene mysteries (and there are other titles beside *Nancy Drew*) are bought by parents because their daughters ask for them; because they are cheap and handy to buy; and because the grownups don't really know what they are buying. They are trash. Read one sometime and see if you can stomach it.

The Bobbsey Twins that hold such a place in younger children's affection's are insipid and all from the same pattern. They do not actually harm children, I suppose, but they do nothing to prepare them for good books. If one could limit the children to two or three, and then stop buying any more, buy them something else, it wouldn't be so bad. Children themselves do not have the cash to buy many books. It must be the grownups who are doing it.

Girls from ten and up are reading not only their own teenage books but all books of adventure, sports, historical adventure, true adventure. They are even reading some adult fiction, some of the things that we used to think of as adult but now have become books for young people.

The number of books these days for girls is endless. I have selected some of the best and most popular authors. It is a pretty safe bet when buying for a girl, if you find yourself at a loss as to what to get, buy a book by an author whose other books you know to be good. The following are all good books, not great maybe, but good.

Favorite Girls' Stories

Kiki Dances. Charlotte Steiner. Doubleday. A very first ballet book in story form, with brief text and very amusing pictures of red-haired Kiki doing her steps. Others equally good: *Kiki Skates, Kiki Goes to Camp, Kiki Loves Music.* Ages 3-8.

Minty's Magic Garden. Story by Charles D. Rice. Pictures by Charles D. Saxon. Dodd. What happened when Minty made three wishes. A very amusing story about a very little girl. Ages 5-8.

Daybreak at Sampey Place. Frances F. Wright. Abingdon. When Aunt Maria left them her house, Judy's family had work making up their minds what to do. This is the fifth story about Judy who lived in the horse-and-buggy days. Girls who are beginning to be readers adore these stories. Others by same author: *Secret of Old Sampey, Surprise at Sampey Place, Poplar Street Park, Eleven Poplar Street.* Ages 7-10.

Middle Sister. Miriam Mason. Macmillan. When the Glosbrenner family moved to Minnesota each child took what she most treasured. Sarah, the middle sister, took her apple tree. A lovely family story, easy to read. Ages 6-8. Another good book by same author: *Sugarbush Family.*

Betsy-Tacy. Maud Hart Lovelace. Crowell. These two five-year-olds, Betsy and Tacy, became inseparable and had many amusing adventures together. Little girls just love this first of several books about the good friends. Others: *Betsy-Tacy and Tib; Over the Big Hill, Down Town.* Ages 8-12.

Seatmates. Mary Reely. Watts. It was hard for Kate to leave the farm, especially since it was in the middle of the year and she would not have a seat mate in school. Before long Kate had a real seat mate. A story of Wisconsin fifty years ago. Easy to read and very popular with little girls. Attractive, too. Ages 8-10.

Good Luck, Mary Ann! Agnes Dean. Abingdon. Mary Ann goes on a week's trial to Aunt Sophia's on Cape Cod. If things go well she will stay all summer. Little girls enjoy this quiet story. Ages 8-10.

Ginnie and Geneva. Catherine Woolley. Morrow. It was Ginnie's first experience in school, in the fourth grade. She hated the teasing Geneva gave her but when she "came back" at her they became very good friends. Ages 8-10. Other books about the same children: *Ginnie and the New Girl; Ginnie Joins In.*

Suzy and the Dog School. Esther MacLellen and Catherine Schroll. Illustrated by Margaret Bradfield. Farrar. Suzy goes to the school for dogs but she flunks everything. However, she makes up for it in a big way. A favorite book. Ages 7-10.

Patchwork Kilt. Mable Watts. Aladdin Books. Biddie who lived on a farm in Scotland liked to dance the highland fling more than anything. The steps the family took to get her a kilt makes a very amusing little girl story. Ages 7-9.

Pink Maple House. Christine Govan. Aladdin Books. Little girls enjoy this happy family story and the adventures of Polly and her friend Jenny in the country. Ages 8-10. Other books about the same little girls and their friend Tilly: *Surprising Summer; Tilly's Strange Secret.*

Ballet for Mary. Written and illustrated by Emma Brock. Knopf. When Mary's father heard she was going to take ballet lessons he almost fell off his chair. He knew the house would come down because everything "Sudden Mary" touched broke. Things weren't quite as bad as the family feared. A very amusing story. Ages 8-10. *Plug Horse Derby* by the same author.

The Family that Grew and Grew. Margaret J. Baker. McGraw. Little did Miss Basingstoke know when she bought the Pekinese that she was starting a family that would include a cat and a stray boy and a toy shop and many friends. Ages 8-10.

Ellen Tebbits. Beverly Cleary. Morrow. Ellen and Austine become good friends when they discover at dancing school that they both have to wear woolen underwear. They have wonderfully good times after that. Ages 8-10.

What Katy Did. Susan Coolidge. Little. Old-fashioned but still appeals to many girls. Others: *What Katy Did at School; What Katy Did Next.* Ages 9-12.

Susannah, A Little Girl of the Mounties. Muriel Denison. Dodd. A little girl tries to become a member of the Canadian North West Mounted Police. Girls love this lively story. *Susannah of the Yukon; Susannah at Boarding School.* Ages 9-12.

Silk and Satin Lane. Esther Wood. Illustrated by Kurt Wiese. Longmans. Ching-Ling gets herself into all sorts of trouble but manages to get out again. A little Chinese tomboy. Each chapter is a separate adventure. Easy to read and very interesting to little girls. Ages 8-10.

A Sod House. Elizabeth Coatsworth. Illustrated by Manning deV. Lee. Macmillan. The German-born Traubel family who believe in freedom, move from Boston to Kentucky, just before the Civil War. Enemies make life a hardship but Ilse is a courageous little girl. Large print and easy to read. Ages 8-10.

Dot for Short. Frieda Friedman. Morrow. A fine story of a happy family that lives under the El in New York. Dot, the ten-year-old heroine, has to solve some pretty tough problems. Ages 8-10. Other titles by same author: *A Sundae with Judy; Carol from the Country.*

Sensible Kate. Doris Gates. Viking. Kate was not pretty but everybody said how sensible she was. She learned that even a freckled redhead can be loved. A warm-hearted story. Ages 9-12.

Adopted Jane. Fern Daringer. Harcourt. An orphan from a Home spends the summer with two different families. They both want her. It is a hard decision to make but she makes the right one. Ages 9-12. Other books by same author: *Stepsister Sally; Mary Montgomery; Rebel.*

Merrylips. Beulah Marie Dix. Macmillan. A little girl held hostage by the Roundheads escapes by dressing as a boy. Girls from two generations have pronounced this good. I know one girl who read it, according to her mother, thirty-five times. Ages 9-12.

All About Majorie. Marion Cumming. Harcourt. A story of Majorie's eighth year in Texas with all the good times. Each chapter is a separate adventure. Ages 9-12.

Sing-Along Sary. Margaret and John T. Moore. Harcourt. Sary Liz earned enough money for three pumpkins at the Fair to buy her brother a fiddle. A charming story of Pennsylvania in the 1850's. Ages 9-12.

The Jennifer Wish. Written and illustrated by Eunice Smith. Bobbs. A delightful story of a delightful family that moved to the country from the city, and the pleasure they found in it—and especially of Jennifer, aged ten, who found a wishing well. Girls love these Jennifer books. Others: *The Jennifer Gift; The Jennifer Prize; Jennifer's Eleven; Jennifer Dances.* Ages 10-12.

All-of-a-Kind Family. Sydney Taylor. Wilcox. A true-to-life story of a first-generation Jewish family on the Lower East Side of New York. A very warm and lovely family picture with their Jewish traditions. *More All-of-a-Kind Family* follows. Ages 9-12.

Island Secret. Mildred Lawrence. Illustrated by Paul Galdone. Harcourt. When father is reported missing in the Far East, Bonnie helps resettle the family on an island in Lake Erie where they own a house. Mysterious doings make life exciting. Bonnie is a charming child. Other girls like her. Ages 2-12. Other titles by same author, all of which are excellent: *Crissey at the Wheel; One Hundred White Horses.*

Little Princess. Frances Hodgson Burnett. Scribner. A little rich girl, orphaned, becomes poor and is badly treated in a boarding school. This is an old favorite. Ages 10-14.

Mrs. Wiggs of the Cabbage Patch. Alice Hegan Rice. Appleton. A both funny and sad story of a poor family that struggles to make the best of things. Mrs. Wiggs is a real character that children love to laugh over. Ages 9-12.

Triumph Clear. Lorraine Beim. Harcourt. A teen-age girl's struggle against the crippling effects of polio at Warm Springs. This is a great favorite with girls from ten years up. Ages 10-14.

Runaway Home. Elinor Lyon. Illustrated by Christine Price. Viking. Cathie didn't know where she came from or who her people were. Following a faint memory of white sand and the sea, she found her way home. A very exciting story in which a Scotch boy and girl help Cathie. Ages 9-12.

Ballet Shoes. Noel Streatfeild. Illustrated by Richard Floethe. Random House. The story of three children who lived in London and studied for careers on the stage. The inside story of stage life appeals to girls. This author is one to remember. Every story she has done is popular, and deservedly. Other titles: *Theatre Shoes; Circus Shoes; Tennis Shoes; Skating Shoes; Family Shoes*. The stories are about different girls, entirely unrelated. Ages 10-14.

Ballet in the Barn. Regina Woody. Ariel. A normal twelve-year-old moves from New York to Martha's Vineyard and finds good teachers of the dance, equal to those in the city. She also finds friendship and tolerance and responsibility. A good dance story for the age that likes them. Ages 10-14.

Little Women. Louisa May Alcott. Little. The still much-read and loved story of Meg, Jo, Beth and Amy. Ages 10-14.

Watch for a Tall White Sail. Margaret Bell. Morrow. A convincing story of a family in Alaska and especially of the sixteen-year-old girl who finds both romance and tragedy. A very lovely story for the early teenager by an excellent author. Others that girls will want to read: *The Totem Casts a Shadow* is a sequel about the same family. *Ride Out the Storm, Love is Forever*. Ages 12-16.

Barrie and Daughter. Rebecca Caudhill. Viking. In a day when women could only either marry or teach school, a Kentucky girl decides to help her father in his store. A good vigorous story with love in it. Ages 12-16.

To Tell Your Love. Mary Stolz. Harper. Anne grew up when her first love was spurned. Others by same author: *The Organdy Cupcakes; The Seagulls Woke Me*. Ages 12-16.

Bright Island. Mabel Robinson. Random House. Thankful Curtis grew up on an island. Her adjustment to a girls' school, so different from what she had known, makes a good story. Ages 12-16.

Tomas and the Red Headed Angel. Marion Garthwaite. Illustrated by Lorence F. Bjorklund. Messner. Tomas, an Indian boy, befriended by Angelita, helps her escape when she defies her father and elopes with the man she loves. Ages 14-16.

North Winds Blow Free. Elizabeth Howard. Morrow. An

adventure-love story during the days of the Underground Railway. Ages 12-16. Other titles: *Peddler's Girl; Candle in the Night; The Road Lies West.*

Fair Adventure. Elizabeth Janet Gray. Illustrated by Alice K. Reischer. Viking. When Page MacNeill graduates from high school it seems as if the family was interested in everything but her. When she fails to win a scholarship to go to college she thinks things are pretty hopeless but she does not know what the summer will bring forth. Ages 12-16. *Meggy Macintosh,* another wonderful story by the same author, is of a Scotch girl who comes to America in 1775. She joins Flora MacDonald. There is romance and brave adventure. Ages 12-16.

Middle Button. Kathryn Worth. Illustrated by Dorothy Bailey. Doubleday. Maggie, who lived in North Carolina in the eighties, had a strange ambition for girls of that time. She wanted to be a doctor. Her parson father and ten brothers and Maggie herself are all colorful characters. This is an extremely popular story with girls, and such a good story, too. Ages 12-16.

They Loved to Laugh, also by Kathryn Worth (Doubleday), is equally popular and good. A story of a Southern Quaker family of the 1830's with five fun-loving boys, and of the girl who came to live with them. There is charming romance in it, just right for the twelve- to fourteen-year-old girls. Ages 12-16.

Lasso Your Heart. Betty Cavanna. Westminster. One of the most popular writers for teen-age girls. Has written a story of life on a Pennsylvania cattle ranch. Prue and Cissy, cousins, learn about friendship, love and courtship, marriage, birth and death, through wholesome family relationships. Other books by Betty Cavanna: *A Girl Can Dream; Going on Sixteen; Paint Box Summer.* Ages 14-16.

Double Date. Rosamond DuJardin. Lippincott. A story of twins, one popular and one a shadow of the other; shadow decides to strike out for herself and develop her own interests.

Wait for Marcy, Marcy Catches Up are two others by the same author. Others: *Practically Seventeen* and *Class Ring.*

Francie. Emily Hahn. Watts. Francie, a typical American teenager, accompanies her father to England and goes to boarding school there. She misses her dates and good times at home but she does get an understanding of the English way of life. Popular with Junior High girls.

Star Dream. Janet Lambert. Dutton. A very popular author with the thirteen-year-olds writes of Dria who spends a summer on her grandmother's farm in Virginia. She learns to train and ride horses so she has a better time than she expected. Many titles by this author. Ages 12-15.

A Girl Called Hank. Amelia Walden. Morrow. The heroine, a basketball star, has her troubles with a new coach, a jealous teammate, and her first romance. A wholesome, interesting story popular with Junior High girls. *Marsha on the Stage, Victory for Jill,* and other titles by this same author.

Only Child. Marguerite Dickson. Longmans. Sixteen-year-old Gwen is used to being the center of attention. When two orphaned cousins come to live at her house, trouble ensues. Good story for early teenagers. Ages 12-16.

Sorority Girl. Anne Emery. Westminster. In her sophomore year in high school, Jean is asked to join a sorority. Thrilled, she accepts. Gradually she sees the drawbacks of the system and finally withdraws from the group. Ages 14-16. *Scarlet Royal* by same author. Also: *Vagabond Summer,* and numerous others popular with girls.

Beany and the Beckoning Road. Lenora Mattingly Weber. Crowell. The sixteen-year-old heroine of this story goes on a motor trip to Denver with her brother, a small nephew, a horse in a trailer, and a remarkable paying passenger. Adventures galore, and a misunderstanding with her boy friend, fill her two weeks' vacation. Ages 12-16. There are many other good books by this fine author.

Innocent Wayfaring. Marchette Chute. Dutton. A perfectly

delightful tale of a runaway girl in fourteenth century England. Ages 12-14.

The Ark. Margot Benary-Isbert. Translated by Clara and Richard Winston. Harcourt. A story of postwar Germany and the Lechow family who, resettled finally in the Western Zone, rebuild their lives with courage. The main character is a girl but both boys and girls love this plucky family and their efforts to live. Ages 12-16.

Step to Music. Phyllis Whitney. Crowell. The coming of the Civil War had a great effect upon Abbie Garrett's family and friends with their divided loyalties and convictions. Abbie grows up through the anxiety and suffering caused by war. Ages 15-17. Other books by this fine writer: *Window for Julie; Star for Ginny; A Long Time Coming, Love Me Love Me Not.*

Seventeenth Summer. Maureen Daly. Dodd. This has been called the "*Little Women* of today." The story of a girl's first falling in love. The girls "eat this one up." It is a splendid book. Ages 12-16.

XII

"Have you a book about the universe?"

FACT BOOKS

YEARS AGO we had many children who didn't read because they didn't like what we had to offer. That kind of child has now become a great library user. It backs up the truth in the overworked adage that there is always a "right book for the right child." There is, I am sure, a right book for every child can we but find it. Even my friend Joe DiGangi who read nothing but battered old Popular Mechanics Magazines (and thereby established a *library habit*) had a right book. The trouble with us adults is we try to give the children *our* choices. A love of reading is built on the child's interest, not on his parent's. A love of reading, as I have mentioned before, is not necessarily a love of the classics, or even a love of fiction, or a love of *many* books. The child's love may be for books, or *a* book, that tells him the facts he yearns for. Bob's love of sailing led him to become a reader. Bill only read what had to do with electricity. Joan's love of art made her study picture books.

Books of information are legion today. Every publisher's list has books on all subjects, from dinosaurs to atoms; biography, history, and how-to-do-it books, because they have found that children "eat them up." There are many, many good books about science, history and the like. I have attempted to suggest only a few, the ones children have enjoyed and found most useful. But if a child is deeply interested in a subject, there are many more books for him to dig and delve in to his heart's content.

Norman stepped inside the library door. He was very little. He had not been to the library by himself before. He was somewhat awed by the older children in there working. I went to meet him. I had to bend over to hear his whispered question. "Have you a book about the universe?" he asked very slowly and distinctly.

Children do not want their facts sugar-coated. They want facts. Period! That is why they love encyclopedias. Many adults have the foolish notion that children cannot be led to "face facts" unless they put a story around them. That is an old-fashioned idea. The result, of course, is a sappy story which no one will read to get the facts. Even in these enlightened times there have been attempts to put facts in story form as if it were a new and enchanting method for getting children to learn. Go back to *Little Rollo*. That is the way he learned geography, by travel. Today we know how children *love to know*.

Probably science is the most popular subject today, all kinds of science. The age of the child doesn't seem to make much difference. Little children are interested in stars and radio and rocks, almost as much as their big brothers and sisters. The first few days of school a first grade (six-year-olds) came to visit the library. At least half of the class wanted to see books about snakes. Only half looked at regular picture books. Why? You tell me. It is the age we live in, I suppose. But it is a *fact* that facts are popular. Here are some good books about science that children like, followed by books on crafts, music, hobbies, etc.

Let's Go Outdoors. Harriet Huntington. Doubleday. Information about snails, turtles, worms, ants, bees, spiders, grasshoppers, etc., illustrated with photographs. Simple brief text.

Ages 6-9. Other books by same author: *Let's Go to the Desert; Let's Go to the Seashore.*

Let's Find Out. A Picture Science Book. Nina and Herman Schneider. Scott. A first book of scientific experiments, things that can be done at home to answer elementary questions about weather, air, etc. Ages 7-9. *Now Try This,* by the same authors, gives information about levers and wheels. Easy experiments. Ages 8-10.

First Book of Science Experiments. Rose Wyler. Watts. Directions for simple experiments with air, water, plants, electricity, chemicals and light, all done with home equipment. Ages 9-12.

Find the Constellations. H. A. Rey. Houghton. Colorful charts and diagrams and information designed to interest children in stars. This book turns many children into star watchers. Ages 8-12.

See for Yourself. Nancy Larrick. Aladdin Books. Easy-to-do experiments for young children, all of them having to do with air and water. For the very youngest. Ages 6-9.

Stars. Herbert Zim and Robert H. Baker. Simon & Schuster. A guide to the constellations, sun, moon, planets and other features of the heavens. Other titles in this same Golden Nature Guide Series: *Insects; Birds; Flowers; Reptiles and Amphibians.*

The Sun. Herbert Zim. Morrow. Why life depends upon heat and light from the sun. Some simple experiments and diagrams. Ages 8-12.

First Book of Electricity. Samuel and Beryl Epstein. Watts. What scientists think electricity is, how it is generated, flows through wires into our homes, and is used in lamps and for machines. Some easy experiments and directions for making a telegraph set. Ages 9-14.

First Electrical Book for Boys. Alfred Morgan. Scribner. For years this has been the most popular book on the subject with the boys. It has been brought up to date. It tells all the things you'd like to know: how batteries work, telephone, telegraph, lights, bells, the electrical system in a car, etc. Ages 10-16. Other books by same author: *First Chemical Book for Boys and Girls; Boy Electrician; Boy's Book of Engines, Motors and Turbines; Aquarium Book for Boys and Girls; Pet Book for Boys and Girls.*

Fun with Chemistry. Mae and Ira Freeman. Random House. A first laboratory book with experiments a child can do at home. Other titles by the same authors: *Fun with Science; Fun with Figures.* Ages 9-12.

All About Volcanoes and Earthquakes. Frederick H. Pough. Illustrated by Kurt Wiese. Random House. What causes a new volcano to start? What makes the ground rumble and shake? The answers to these and other questions children ask are here, written simply and interestingly. Ages 9-14. *All About Dinosaurs; All About Insects,* and many others in series.

Earth's Adventures. Carroll Lane Fenton. Day. An interesting nontechnical geology for children, telling of the past changes in the earth's surface and of those going on now. A fascinating account of the solar system, volcanoes and the making of rocks. The chapters *sound* interesting: Rocks Once Hot; How Valleys Grow Old; Rain and Rivers Destroy, etc. Ages 10-16. Other titles by this author: *Life Long Ago:* the story of fossils; *Wild Folk at the Pond; Along Nature's Highway; Plants That Feed Us:* The story of Grains and Vegetables.

Field Book of Common Rocks and Minerals. Frederic Loomis. Putnam. For identifying the rocks and minerals of the United States. A very good book for a family to own. All ages. Many titles in this exciting series.

First Book of Stones. M. B. Cormack. Watts. Characteristics, origin and location of many types of minerals with some simple experiments. A real beginning book on stones. Ages 8-12. *First Book of Plants; First Book of Trees; First Book of Sea Shells,* and many other titles in this excellent series.

Everyday Weather and How It Works. Herman Schneider. McGraw. One of the most popular books about weather. When children used it in school the entire class wanted to buy copies to have at home. You might say that it has made weather popular. The what, why, and how of weather with instructions for making a home weather map, cloud seeding, rainmaking, and many easy experiments. Other books by same author: *More Power to You:* A Short History of Power from the Windmill to the Atom. Ages 10-15.

Dinosaurs. Herbert Zim. Morrow. Describes many kinds of dinosaurs throughout the ages and tells how they changed. Large clear type and easy to read. Ages 9-14.

True Book of Dinosaurs. Mary Lou Clark. Children's Press. The very simplest, and a very attractive, book on the subject. Very little children can enjoy it by themselves. Ages 6-10. *True Books of Shells* and many other titles in The True Book Series.

Golden Treasury of Natural History. Bertha M. Parker. Simon & Schuster. One of the most gorgeous and fascinating books on natural science, beginning with dinosaurs and discussing insects, fishes, trees, plants, flowers and fruits as well as minerals and planets. Children adore this large book illustrated in color. No family should be without one. Ages 8-16.

What Butterfly Is It? Anna Pistorius. Wilcox. Fifty-four of the best-known butterflies are shown here in lifelike color. Other books by same author: *What Wildflower Is It? What Tree Is It?* Ages 7-10.

First Book of Snakes. John Hoke. Watts. How to identify some of the most common snakes and the poisonous ones, and all about their habits. Ages 7-10. *First Book of Prehistoric Animals; First Book of Bugs; First Book of Birds,* and many other titles in this series.

Snakes. Herbert Zim. Morrow. How the North American snakes produce their young, how they grow, why they are valuable, etc. The type is nice and big and the sentences are easy to read. A very popular book with youngsters. Ages 9-15.

Boy's Book of Snakes: How to Recognize and Understand Them. Percy Morris. Ronald. Nonpoisonous and poisonous snakes of the country, described. A lot of misinformation is disposed of and true facts given. Boys like this book very much and seem to find it most useful. Ages 12-16.

Birds and Their Nests. Olive L. Earle. Morrow. Forty-two varieties of birds and their nests, from the ostrich to the woodpecker, are presented. A very attractive little book for children from 8-12.

Introduction to Birds. John Kieran. Illustrated by Don Eckleberry. Garden City. Characteristics and habits of the common birds on lawns and in fields and woods. Large beautiful book. Ages 10-15.

Birds in Your Garden. Margaret McKenny. University of Minnesota Press. How to attract birds, provide homes, characteristics of birds—almost everything you need to know, in fact, in this big, beautiful book. Children have found it very interesting. Ages 8 and up.

Great Whales. Herbert Zim. Illustrated by James Gordon Irving. Morrow. Children these days have a great interest in whales, and there has been very little for them to read. This book tells many interesting facts about them: how deep they can dive, do they see and hear, what do they fear, how fast can they swim, etc. All the facts simply explained. Large type. Excellent drawings. Ages 7-9.

What's Inside of Me. Herbert Zim. Morrow. A book that helps children understand their bodies. Many drawings, easy text, makes this a useful book for younger children. It is very popular with children. Ages 7-10.

Wonders of the Human Body. Anthony Ravielli. Viking. A perfectly marvelous book of human anatomy illustrated with beautiful drawings. Ages 10-16.

Growing Up. The story of how we become alive and are born and grow up. Karl De Schweinitz. Macmillan. First published in 1928, this book is still one of the most useful books for parents and for older children. A clear, direct book of sex instruction for older children. Ages 14-16.

The Wonderful Story of How You Were Born. Sidonie Gruenberg. Garden City. The author has presented the facts of life in such a normal, healthy way that the things that puzzle children will be clear and unembarrassing. (All ages).

How Your Body Works. Herman and Nina Schneider. Scott. First part of the book deals with the digestive processes; the second part with the senses and nervous system. Written simply so that children can understand it. Ages 9-12.

What's Inside of Engines. Herbert Zim. Morrow. An explanation with words and pictures of what actually goes on inside of engines: gasoline, diesel, steam turbine, jet, rocket and atomic pile. Why, *I* can almost understand it, it is that simple! Large type is used for the simple explanation, then in fine type there is more detailed information for an adult to fill in the gaps. Ages 8-12.

In spite of the many jokes about father and the electric train, little boys do love them. There have been a couple of good books about them, and they are in great demand.

Boys' Book of Model Railroading. Raymond Yates. Harper. How model railroads are constructed and how the owner of a set can get the most fun out of them. Instructions are provided for setting up model railroad stations and towns, and creating scenery out of inexpensive materials. One chapter explains the electrical principles involved. Ages 10-16.

How to Improve Your Model Railroading. Raymond Yates. Harper. How to make additional accessories from materials at home. Ages 10-16.

Television Works Like This. Jeanne and Robert Bendick. McGraw. One of the few books about television for children. This has chapters on colored television. Ages 12-16.

The Man in the Manhole and the Fix-It Man. Juniper Sage. Scott. A picture book about the men who work under the city, and other repair men. Ages 6-8.

The First Book of Space Travel. Written and illustrated by

Jeanne Bendict. Watts. Facts about a space's size, shape and place lead up to the rocket and its workings. Description of a space suit, a space station, and what you might see on a trip to the moon. A section on "Space Chatter," the terminology used, makes lots of fun. Ages 9-14.

By Space Ship to the Moon. Jack Coggins and Fletcher Pratt. Random House. The most probable steps man will take for space travel: reasons, first rocket and station for it, clothing to be worn, conditions that probably will be found. Illustrated with many pictures. A large flat book. Very popular with boys. Ages 10-16. Another book by same authors: *Rockets, Jets, Guided Missiles and Space Ships,* in which is explained the history and advance made in these marvels. Full color pictures.

Jets of the World. C. B. Colby. Coward. In one volume the author has gathered the top jets of all the nations. Illustrated with photographs. Ages 8-10. Children are fascinated by the pictures in this book and the others in the series. Others are: *Our Fighting Jets; Ships of our Navy; Wings of our Air Force; Wings of our Navy.*

Pet Book for Boys and Girls. Alfred Morgan. Scribner. One of the most popular books about pets with children. Includes a chapter on hamsters. Ages 8-12.

Parrakeets. Herbert Zim. Morrow. How to raise, train and breed parrakeets. The text and illustrations explain how to feed them and the best kinds of food to give them, what sort of a cage they should have, and how to teach them to talk, etc. A very popular book these days when so many children have parrakeets and there is not much material on them. Ages 12-16.

Honeybee. Mary Adrian. Holiday. An easy science book, very attractive, telling simply about the life in the hive. Very interesting to young children. Ages 5-10.

Codes and Secret Writing. Herbert Zim. Morrow. Boys especially are interested in codes. This tells about progressively more difficult codes and how to break them. It includes a section on secret writing and invisible inks.

American Boys' Book of Signs, Signals and Symbols, with 362 illustrations by the author. Daniel Beard. Lippincott. This is a very popular book in spite of its age. It includes not only the regular type of codes but danger signs, trail signs, deaf-and-dumb alphabet, Indian signs, railway signals. In fact, it even includes a description of hobo signs. A very fascinating book. Ages 10-16.

Tim and the Toolchest. Jerrold Beim. Morrow. Tim's Dad shows him how to use tools. A story. Ages 6-8.

Woodworking. Written and illustrated by Roger Lewis. Knopf. Easy to follow directions for making simple useful objects and how to use the basic woodworking tools. Ages 8-10.

The Boy Mechanic. Popular Mechanics Press. This edition replaces the original four-volume set of books with material from Popular Mechanics Magazine, so popular with boys. Covers all kinds of handicraft. Very alluring to boys of all ages.

Tools In Your Life. Irving Adler. Day. The story of tools from the Old Stone Age to the present, including power. Ages 11 up. Other titles: *Time in Your Life, Fire in Your Life.*

The Art of Chinese Paper Folding For Young and Old. Mei-ying Sung. Harcourt. I got the surprise of my life when this book became so popular. In fact, there was a waiting list of boys. I remember thinking when I bought one copy that it would be the rare child who would use it. Never was I more wrong. The teachers began to complain; in fact, even asked me to suppress the book. You see, it tells how to make, among other fascinating things, water bombs. Every home with a boy or girl needs this book. All ages.

The Story of Painting for Young People from Cave Painting to Modern Times. Horst W. and Dora J. Janson. Abrams. I am not pretending that this is popular with all children. But I have noticed many children, both boys and girls, who are interested in art books. This is one of the finest for young people. It is interestingly written. The selection of paintings are those interesting to children. A big, beautiful book. Ages 12-16.

Photography for Basic Cameras. William Gottlieb. Knopf. Explains how to make good pictures. Describes cameras most suitable for young folks, what film to buy, how to compose a picture, etc. Ages 9-14.

The First Book of Photography. John Hoke. Watts. More detailed than the above photography book. It includes a brief history of photography, uses of photography, as well as basic information concerning the camera itself. Ages 10-14.

American Folk Songs for Christmas. Ruth P. Seeger, Barbara Cooney. Doubleday. More than fifty American folk songs based on Christmas themes. Nice family book. For everybody.

Stories from Great Metropolitan Operas. Helen Dike. Illustrated by Gustaf Tenggren. Random House. The plots and stories of twenty-five operas. The best book on the subject that I know of for children. Ages 12-16.

The Fireside Book of Folk Songs. Margaret B. Boni. Arranged for the piano by Norman Lloyd. Illustrated by Alice and Martin Provensen. Simon & Schuster. A beautiful book to look at and an extremely useful one. Intended for family and group singing of the old favorites. 147 songs. (Family).

The First Book of Puppets. Maurice Jagendorf. Watts. Instructions on how to make different kinds of puppets, and for acting, staging and the plays themselves. Ages 8-12.

Easy Puppets. Gertrude Pels. Crowell. Making and using hand puppets. Illustrated by Albert Pels. An easy book for a child to read to himself showing how he can construct and operate puppets made from things at hand. Directions for making papier mâché heads included. A very popular "first" book. Ages 8-14.

The First Book of Ballet. Noel Streatfeild. Watts. All the beginning dancer needs to know about the ballet, from its history to the steps. Ages 8-12.

Fun with Ballet. Mae Freeman. Random House. Elementary instruction in ballet dancing. Ages 10-16.

The First Book of Magic. Edward Stoddard. Watts. Easy-to-follow directions for the best and simplest tricks for beginners. All materials needed can be found at home. Tells how to put on a magic show. Ages 9-12. Boys are crazy over magic.

Fun with Magic. Joseph Leeming. Lippincott. How to make magic equipment, how to perform many tricks, and how to give successful shows. Ages 10-16. A very well-liked book on the subject.

Boxing for Boys. Written and illustrated by Donald K. Silks. Knopf. Footwork, punches, offensive and defensive strategy, and the simplest equipment needs are covered. Ages 9-14.

The First Book of Sailing. Marion M. Lineaweaver. Watts. A guide for beginning sailors. Picture and text tell essential knots and parts of a boat and what they are called. Tells all that is necessary for good seamanship. Ages 10-15.

First Fish: What you should know to catch him. Written and illustrated by C. B. Colby. Coward. Information on various kinds of fish, where to find them, how to catch and cook them. Ages 8-14.

Let's Fish. Written and illustrated by Harry Zarchy. Knopf. A guide to fresh and salt water: equipment, casting, bait, characteristics of various fish, tackle making and repair, etc. For older boys. Ages 14-16.

Boys' Treasury of Things to Do. Caroline Horowitz. Hart. A Good Time book for children, telling of many activities. Ages 8-12. *Girls' Treasury of Things to Do. Little Girls' Treasury of Things to Do. Young Boys' Treasury of Things to Do.* Things to do at parties, when you're in bed, etc.

The Golden Geography Book. A child's introduction to the world. Elsa Jane Werner. Pictures by Cornelius DeWitt.

Simon & Schuster. Presents the world with more than three hundred full-color paintings. Describes life in all kinds of regions. Large attractive map at back. Children adore this book and want to own their own copies. Ages 8-10.

Picture Books of the States. (One for each State.) Written by Bernadine Bailey. Whitman. Very popular little books illustrated in color, brief text, easy to read. An introduction to our country. Ages 8-10.

Weapons. Written and illustrated by Edward Tunis. World Book. An exquisite, large book showing with black-and-white line drawings, in great detail, the weapons of the world from the beginning, briefly giving interesting facts about them and the people who used them. Another equally wonderful book by same author-illustrator: *Wheels,* a history of transportation. An earlier one *Oars, Sails, and Steam* does for water what *Wheels* does for land. Wonderful books to own. All ages.

I would like to give special mention to an author, and list a few of his titles, because he has done so much for young people, especially boys, in giving them true pictures of many of the occupations in our country today. And he has told them so dramatically in words and photographs that his books are among the most popular with Junior High age children.

The Courage and the Glory, true stories of great American heroes during World War II. John J. Floherty. Lippincott. *Flowing Gold, Romance of the Oil Fields; Inside the F.B.I.,* (naturally, one of his most popular books); *Men Against Crime,* battle against counterfeiters; *Men Without Fear,* dangerous occupations; *Sentries of Sea,* Lighthouse Service; *Youth and the Sea,* Merchant Marine; *Guardians of the Coast,* Coast Guard.

Another author who has done a great deal for boys is Commander Edward Ellsberg.

On the Bottom. An account of the raising of a submarine. Commander Edward Ellsberg. Dodd. *Thirty Fathoms Deep.* Salvaging for sunken treasure.

"Is there anyone dead living here?"

Biographies

That question the little boy asked when he delivered flowers is the question we have to ask ourselves about the many biographies that are being written today. Are these stories about people real? Do they come alive?

Naturally, children like best the stories about people who led lives that would be exciting to a child. It is normal that Buffalo Bill, Kit Carson, John Paul Jones and Davy Crockett should be heroes. Davy never was popular until Walt Disney immortalized him. Now we can't get enough of him. Publishers are turning out biographies by the dozen. Some will be read because of the subject. Some will be relegated to libraries for reference. Some are well written. Some are not. Some are really good biographies and some are useful only as easy reading and lure to the boy who doesn't like to read. Some are more fictionized than others. Some are by famous authors and some are by unknown writers. The fact that the author is famous doesn't necessarily mean he has written a good book for children. The unknown writer may have loved his subject so much that he did a splendid job. Some biographies are really great. For the most part, they are not. Just good.

The real value in this flood of "true stories" today is in the bait they offer the boys and girls who have heretofore not enjoyed reading. I know one boy who refuses gifts of any books except biographies and histories. He wouldn't be bothered reading fiction, yet he reads a great deal.

No hero is as popular with children as Abraham Lincoln. Children read about him all the year round, not just in February.

Abraham Lincoln. Ingri and Edgar d'Aulaire. Doubleday. Caldecott Medal book. A picture book with all the essential facts about Lincoln's life from childhood to the end of the Civil War. Ages 7-9. Other biographies by the same authors: *George Washington, Benjamin Franklin, Buffalo Bill, Pocahontas, Columbus.*

The Columbus Story. Alice Dalgliesh. Illustrated by Leo Politi. Scribner. This is a gorgeous story of Columbus for little children following the main adventures of his life, from the time he was a boy up to the start of his second voyage. The author and artist have done a superb job. Wonderful to read aloud. Certainly nothing has been done so well about Columbus for little children before. Ages 6-10.

Little Brother of the Wilderness. The story of Johnny Appleseed. Meridel LeSueur. Knopf. A wonderfully told story of the man who loved apple trees and made it his life work to plant them through America. Ages 7-10.

Squanto, Friend of the White Man. Clyde Bulla. Crowell. A beautiful story of the Indian who was a friend and helper of the Pilgrims, and of his adventures here and in England, his happiness and the great tragedy when he returned to find his people gone. Easy reading. Ages 8-10.

Joan of Arc. Written and illustrated by Boutet de Monvel. Century. A very popular picture-book biography of The Maid. A classic. Ages 9-14.

Early American: The Story of Paul Revere. Mildred Pace. Scribner. A very readable and dramatic account of the life and times of the great silversmith, bell maker and patriot. The author brings out the real man and his contribution, and tells it so interestingly that children love to read it. Ages 10-14.

Geronimo. The Last Apache War Chief. Edgar Wyatt. Illustrated by Allan Houser. McGraw. How he came to hate the white man, how he was hunted for years and finally gave up. This is a very readable book and unusually popular with children. Ages 9-12. Another book by the same author: *Cochise, Apache Warrior and Statesman.*

Leif Ericksson. First Voyager to America. Katherine B. Shippen. Harper. A brief but excellent biography of the early explorer, simply written with action and adventure. Ages 11-15.

Magellan, First Around the World. Ronald Syme. Morrow. Heroic story of the first man to sail around the world, with storms, mutiny and starvation. Ages 9-14. Other titles by same author: *Columbus, LaSalle, Cortes, Champlain.*

Clara Barton. Mildred M. Pace. Illustrated by Robert Ball. Scribner. Well written, interesting and easy to read, it shows Clara Barton with her tireless energy, her desire to help humanity, and her work on the Civil War battlefields and other places. Girls are particularly interested in nurses. Ages 9-14.

Indian Captive: The Story of Mary Jamison. Written and illustrated by Lois Lenski. Lippincott. One of the most popular true stories with twelve- to fourteen-year-olds is this life of the white child who was captured by the Indians. The background is authentic but never intrudes. Ages 12-16.

Tree Toad: Adventures of the Kid Brother. Robert H. Davis. Illustrated by Robert McCloskey. Lippincott. A humorous account of the boyhood pranks of the author and his ingenious brother. Boys laugh loud and long over this story. Ages 12-16.

America's Ethan Allen. Stewart H. Holbrook. Pictures by Lynd Ward. Houghton. A rousing story of a great American patriot, hero of Fort Ticonderoga. A short story illustrated with lovely colored pictures. Ages 14-16.

Haym Solomon, Son of Liberty. Howard M. Fast. Messner. A moving and not too well-known story of a Polish Jew immigrant who built up a fortune and devoted it to the service of his country during the Revolution. Very readable and popular. Ages 12-16.

Knight of the Sea: The Story of Stephen Decatur. Harcourt. Corinne Lowe. A romantic portrait of the daring sea fighter who was known best for his fight with the Barbary Pirates. The adventure appeals to the boys. Ages 14-16.

Amos Fortune, Freeman. Elizabeth Yates. Aladdin Books. Newberry Medal, 1951. A magnificent story of an African prince, made a slave, who eventually purchased his own freedom. He became a worthwhile citizen and did a great deal for his community. This is really a great book and it is so wonderful that the children recognize this and love it. Ages 11-16.

The Most Talked-about Series

There is a perfect flood of series books these days, especially in the realm of biography and history. The most talked-about one is *The Landmark Series,* published by Random House. It was the first, and is the most advertised and probably the most read. The children have come to believe that any *Landmark* book is good. They come to the library and ask for "another Landmark." Some titles are not as popular as others, of course, depending on the subject. The most popular titles are the frontier biographies, and those of inventors and historic figures.

Close runners-up for popularity, especially with the younger children, are what they call "the little orange books," *The Childhood of Famous Americans* series published by Bobbs Merrill. There must be a hundred and fifty titles of these little books, easy to read, attractive in appearance, and in great demand for easy reading as much as for biography. Naturally, here, too, some characters are more popular than others. In fact, there are many that do not appeal because their lives lacked a certain drama that children are looking for.

The *Signature Books* published by Grosset are very popular and excellent for children who do not read well. A teacher interested in reading experimented with the different biographies. She found that children preferred the *Signature Books* when put to the test, because of the ease with which they could read them, the dramatic beginnings, and, apparently, the reality of the subjects. As one boy said of one hero, "He makes me think of my pop when he blows his top."

The *Landmark* books are more attractive in space, type and decoration, and especially the outside of the book. The *Childhood of Famous Americans* series has the advantage of a very attractive size; children like little books. All the series cover pretty much the same subjects except that *Landmark* has gone into history too, and into *World Landmark* books which have to do with heroes of other countries and some historic events in other parts of the world. *Signatures* are strictly biographical. The *Childhood* series has many more subjects, many more women, and many people less well known.

Landmark books, for the most part, have been written by well-known writers of adult books. *Signature Books* are written by well-known writers in the juvenile field. With the *Childhood* series, many authors have done many books. Other publishers are developing lines of biographies but they do not name them as series.

Landmark Books. Random House. Covers United States history from Exploration through Colonial Period, Revolutionary War, National Development after it, Westward Expansion, Civil War period up to 1918, then to the present. This includes biographies of people during each period, and special events. *World Landmarks* include *Alexander the Great, The Crusades, etc.* For ages 10-16.

Signature Books. Edited by Enid Meadowcroft. Grosset. Biographies of well-known American heroes. For ages 9-15.

Childhood of Famous Americans. Bobbs. For ages 8-12. Covers the heroes of American History and many other people, men and women, who have made a contribution in literary, political, creative inventive things. Excellent for the older child who is having reading trouble, and for the younger readers.

All About Series. Random House. Large, attractive books about different kinds of science, each by a different author. Easy to understand. Ages 8-14.

First Books. Watts. "First" books on many and varied subjects. Attractive. Easy to understand. Many authors. Ages 8-14.

Real Books. Garden City. Inexpensive, easy-to-read books on many subjects. Ages 8-14.

What is the best kind of encyclopedia?

A word should be said about encyclopedias. So many parents ask "Which is the best encyclopedia?" I remember an author of dog stories who came to school to talk to the children. They were all agog over this wonderful man. He stepped out over the footlights in the auditorium and asked "What is the best kind of dog to own?" Each and every one of those kids sucked in his breath. "The kind you have," he finished. Breathing became normal.

It is almost like that with encyclopedias. The one you have is good unless it is too old. And even the old encyclopedias have their uses. Or the one the salesman sells you when your resistance is weak, that could be all right for you too. Nothing is lost, although it is true that there are some thought to be better than others.

The two best-known encyclopedias for children are:

World Book. Field Enterprises. 19 volumes. Useful in elementary grades and also in Junior High School. Kept up to date with supplements, and then revised at each new printing. If you have not seen the newer editions you have no idea how attractive they are, vastly superior in text, looks, illustrations from the early sets. Very popular with children because of arrangement in straight alphabetical style with cross-references. Ages 8-16.

Compton's Pictured Encyclopedia. Compton Co. This is an excellent set of books, arranged alphabetically with broad articles and a detailed fact index at the back of each volume for the little articles and references. Very attractive. Continually revised. It looks a little easier to read than *World Book.* Actually, they are about the same. Ages 8-16.

One word about buying an encyclopedia. Never let a salesman tell you you have to have one. When your child begins to want information at home, for his own pleasure, for his school work, then is the time to buy an encyclopedia. If you buy one when your child is only two or three (and some people have been convinced that they are not doing right by their children unless they do) the material, or some of it, is out of date before the child is old enough to need it.

And a word about sets of books. Many sets are on the market, sets that have all the stories your child should know, according to the salesman. If you wish to spend the money for them, knowing that they will not be used for many years, then—fine. Usually the first volume with stories for the youngest child is worn to a frazzle. But when the child is old enough to read to himself, the big heavy volumes of a set, or the fine print, or the too-much-of-a-muchness discourages the older child. He prefers individual books. Think how many little books the price of a set of books would buy! And what fun it is to have them separate in their attractive format!

The World Almanac. World Telegram. You can buy it at a newstand for comparatively little, and it is one of the most useful reference books you can have in the house. It answers almost all the questions.

Columbia One-Volume Encyclopedia. Columbia University. One of the best buys for your money. You'll be surprised how much information is given in that one large volume. Good for family use.

XIII

"I get enough reading in school."

BOOKS FOR NONREADERS

How many times do we say to ourselves, "How terrible it must be to be blind!" Or, "What a handicap to be deaf!" But have you ever really stopped to think what it would be like in the world today to be unable to read? Think of driving along the road unable to read the signs of direction, interesting placards, or even Burma Shave "ads." To be unable to read bus or trolley or subway signs, street names, business names. To go into a restaurant and not know what the menu says. To be unable to vote, drive a car, or even join the army. How many jobs can you think of that could be filled with a person unable to read? Yet there are many grown people who cannot read a word. A reading teacher told me of a man whom she was teaching at a reading clinic. He couldn't read a word. He worked as a furrier and had a family. He had been one of a large family of children. The father used to stand over them with a strap to make them study. His brothers and sisters tried to help him but his terror blocked any chance he had of learning to read. Eventually he ran away from home. After he married and had a family of his own he decided to try once more to learn to read. The teacher asked him how he managed to get along without reading. "Well," he said, "I have learned to follow crowds in the subway. In a restaurant I look around to see what other people are eating, or I say 'What's good today?' or I order ham and eggs." She suggested that he might like to take his books home to study. "Oh, no," he said hastily, "My children don't know I can't read, and I am ashamed to have them find out."

Jimmy had me completely fooled. He was a new boy in the third grade. He came to the library daily, always asking for books by name. They were always good books, popular books, books other children were reading. I didn't take the trouble to hear him read because he seemed to know what he wanted. My only thought was "What a precocious boy!" One day he was in with his class. He was what we call a wanderer. He went from this to that in a nuisancy fashion. I made some remark to his teacher. "His trouble," she said, "is that he can't read." He literally couldn't read a word. He was unusually intelligent. He knew book names, and he terribly wanted to be like the others. Jimmy was given special help, and bit by bit he learned to read. At first it was like chiseling a design out of marble; slowly, slowly something took shape. Finally, he knew how to read. By the time he was in the sixth grade he was reading way above the grade level. Not only that, but, miraculously, he *loved* to read. He loved books. When we had our book sale he bought books for his whole family for Christmas.

Doris came to the library one day. She looked miserable. She slumped as she came in and went to the picture-book section. She was too old to be looking at picture books. I asked if I could help her. "I don't read very well," she said with real anguish. We spent a long time trying books. It so happened that Emma Brock's *Here Comes Kristie* was new and on our shelves. I shall never cease being grateful for that book. It was interesting, it was easy to read, and more than that, it looked like a real book. Doris could read it. She literally flushed with pleasure. Each time she came to the library we took time to find more books she could read. It was amazing how many she read that spring. After this had been going on for several weeks her mother, whom I had never met, stopped by to tell me what reading meant to Doris. "That first time she brought a book home," said her mother, "she wanted to read in bed. She had just discovered that people read for pleasure."

I was invited to a fourth-grade classroom to hear the children read some poems they had written. I sat down beside Sandra who read two delightful poems. I peeked over her shoulder and was simply amazed at what I saw. It looked like Shakespearean English. This is what I saw:

> that is byooty
> A teenkleng streem roning throo the wud's wat with
> doo. That is byooty.
>
> A ciled playing by a brak lafing at the fish that
> dart throo the wather that is byooty.
>
> The sun coming up behined a snow c apt mootn.
> Look for a lovly thing and you will fined it.
> It is not fur. It will navr be for.

I was so surprised at what I saw I made haste to ask the teacher about the child. "She just resists learning to read and spell," said the teacher. "She'll go to any trouble to avoid it." Sandra was a challenge. Beautiful words were the answer. We sat down with *In My Mother's House.* It was a slow process demanding patience, but it was also a joyful one. She would read one sentence, then trail off into a dreamy silence. Then she would sigh, "Now isn't that beautiful?" Or, "What a lovely picture!" A word picture, she meant. I brought out *The Oak Tree House,* of Katherine Gibson's, Howard Pyle's *Wonder Clock.* Now, I'm not a teacher of reading. I wouldn't know how to begin to do it. What I could do with her and Doris and Jimmy was to make them want to read, or at least stimulate some little germ of desire. It was the beauty of words that finally got Sandra. Once the desire is born, with special help these children do learn to read.

One of the most interesting things I have had to do was to work with a special group of nonreading children, bright children who we knew would read eventually. My special part in their lives was to keep them interested in books and the library until they knew how to read, to have them see that books are fun. Otherwise there would have been a gap in their lives, and by the time they could read they might have lost interest. It was great fun and satisfaction. What I found was what every reading teacher knows, that reading was not their main problem. There were many reasons why they couldn't read. Some of them were very immature and couldn't listen very long. I would have to stop in the middle of a story to let them have some kind of activity, like playing a story, and then go back to the book. Pathetically they called their "club" the "Reading-Is-Fun Club." Not one of them could read. A few had physical defects. Karl, whose hearing was not good, was just crazy to read. Ann had bad sight only recently discovered. Several had emotional problems, as a result of home troubles.

Parents have a tendency to blame schools for these reading problems, and schools are likely to blame homes. Each has a share, no doubt, in the trouble. There are things each can do to help these children who want, more than anything, to read. They want to read for many reasons, but especially to be like other people. We grownups haven't been to school for a long time and have forgotten what it is like. Most of us are really interested in helping our children even if we seem, sometimes, to be doing the wrong things. The demand is proved by the very fact that so many commercial firms have put on the market lots of short cuts for parents to help their children learn: records, work books, games—all designed to teach the child to read in short order. There is no easy road for the child who has a problem, either emotional or physical, and usually we have to go back farther to find the real cause of the trouble.

Do you remember the old Ford joke about the old couple out driving one Sunday with their horse and buggy? A car came along and scared the horse. The driver of the car came over to the couple and said, "May I lead your horse past?" The old man replied, "You take the old woman past. I can get the horse by all right." I sometimes feel that the real problem in reading is with us grownups. If someone would lead us past, the children would get along all right.

There are many reasons why children do not learn to read. Often there is a foreign background which has resulted in a limited vocabulary. Sometimes it is poor cultural background. Maybe, as I have mentioned before, the child comes from a nonreading family. Some children never see books until they come to school. Books have not been part of their lives. No books at home. No one around looking at books. No one telling stories to them when they are babies, or showing them picture books or teaching them Mother Goose Rhymes.

For some there are the emotional problems I spoke of, real disturbances that prevent their learning to read. Parents disagree at home. No mother's care. One child I know who had reading problems had been handed from nurse to nurse the first four years of his life. Bad living habits affect some. I am thinking now of all the children in crowded apartments who sit up late because they sleep in the room where the family sits. Television, radio, street noises, poor diet—oh, it might be a number of things.

A very unusual story appeared in a mystery-story magazine. It was called "Teacher, Do You Know What?" The whole plot was worked out in the conversation between a six-year-old girl and her teacher. On the days the little girl came to school without her breakfast because of trouble at home—her hair uncombed, not properly dressed—on those days she couldn't remember her words. But once in a while when things were right at home between mother and father, then the little girl was bright and eager and could remember her lessons. The story was written by a teacher who knew from experience how it goes with children.

Perhaps there are physical defects yet undiscovered. I have a friend who has been deaf for as long as she remembers. But no one discovered it until she was five, then they only knew she did not come when she was called, and she knew she had to work hard to keep up with other children.

One of the problems in teaching the slightly older children to read is the lack of suitable material. The pre-primers and simple books are too babyish. Brian was having great difficulty learning to read—he had real emotional problems at home. At the same time he was completely absorbed in making space ships. One day when his teacher was hearing him read he looked up at her. "Isn't it ridiculous? I use words like stratosphere and gravity, but I have to read 'The bunny hopped, hopped, hopped.' I wouldn't even *say* bunny, I'd say rabbit."

All children want to read. They may not want to read what we want them to, but they do want to read. It is up to us to provide books and opportunity for all kinds of children. It also takes friendliness, patience, enthusiasm and leisure on our parts to promote it with the child who can't read, the child who is just beginning, and the child who just plain doesn't read when we think he should.

As a student librarian once said at the end of her stay, "Well, I have learned one thing, put first things first." If what we are after is to help children find joy in books, then we must put that before some other things.

I am suggesting books for three kinds of readers here: The young beginning reader, who needs lots of easy books for practice; the slightly older child who is having difficulty in learning; the child who doesn't like to read for pleasure.

"I didn't know a big book could be so easy," John said,

you'll remember, when he saw *Kit and Kat* by Lucy Fitch Perkins.

I would like to say just a word about "easy" books. Picture books, for the most part, are not easy to read. That is, not necessarily so. They are the books for the "read-to" age. The words do not need to be easy to read, for most children understand much bigger words than they can read for a long time. There are some picture books, however, that are easy, and they will be listed. Another thing that sometimes fools us is large type. Some publishers seem to think that putting a story into great big type automatically makes it easy to read. The story may be a simple one. The words may not be so difficult. But order of words sometimes throws a beginning reader off. A story that starts "Snuggled up close to its mother's side" presents several difficulties. It is a pretty tough beginning for a child who doesn't know very much about reading. Words may be simple but the idea a subtle one. I believe the classic example of that is "The boy is father to the man." I have noticed that so many of the joke and riddle books that entice little children are too difficult for them to understand. They read the words so hopefully aloud to a friend and then the blank look comes over their faces. What does it mean?

When picking out a book for a youngster to read to himself there are several things we should think of. Simple sentences. Good spacing of the page so that it looks readable. So many times children take one look at a page of type and say "That is too hard for me." It may not be too hard at all but it surely looks dull. Pictures breaking up a page of type help. Some grownups may think this is all sheer foolishness, but believe me, it is important.

Books for Beginners

Kit and Kat. Lucy Fitch Perkins. Houghton. The large edition because it is so much more attractive. Children get great joy out of this simple story because they can actually read it. Ages 6-8. It is just about as simple as a pre-primer and much more exciting.

The Disney Readers, so-called by the children because they are illustrated by Disney pictures. D. C. Heath. These little books are very popular with not only beginning readers, but with older children who are having difficulties. They begin with titles like *Here We Are, Donald Duck and His Nephews, Water Babies, Bambi, Dumbo, Mickey Never Fails, Donald Duck and His Friends, Little Pig's Picnic.* They are written by excellent authors and are absolutely infallible in helping beginning readers and those who are having reading trouble. Age 6 and up.

Joan Wanted a Kitty. Jane B. Gemmill. Illustrated by Marguerite De Angeli. Winston. Joan was happy when she found a bedraggled kitty. Large type. Short sentences. Perfect for beginning reader. Age 6 and up.

The True Book Series. Children's Press. These wonderfully easy-to-read books on a variety of subjects are invaluable for little children to read and some are good for the older children having trouble. For the beginner I would suggest *The True Book of Animal Babies, The Circus, Health, Indians, Insects, Plants We Know, Policemen and Firemen, Our Post Office, Trees.* A little more difficult are the following: *Animals of Small Pond, Birds We Know, Farm Animals, Little Eskimos, Pebbles and Shells, Tools for Building, Weeds and Wildflowers.* They are all nicely illustrated and written by people who know how children read.

Tiny Toosey's Birthday. Mabel G. La Rue. Houghton. A delightful book for the young reader. It is as simple as a preprimer but has a little story and nice humor. Illustrations are interesting to children, too. Ages 6-8.

Willie's Adventures. Margaret Wise Brown. Scott. Three little stories about Willie, so easy to read. The book is a nice small size that children love. Ages 6-8.

Little Jonathan. Miriam Mason. Macmillan. Jonathan had twelve older brothers and sisters. They said he was too little to do anything until he proved he wasn't. A pioneer story, attractive and easy to read. Other easy-to-read stories by same author: *Matilda and Her Family, Susannah, The Pioneer Cow, Timothy Had Ideas.*

Tippy. Sally Scott. Harcourt. A kitten left alone goes off to find a new home. Appeals to little children, and they can read it. Ages 6-10.

Little Fisherman. Margaret Wise Brown. Scott. Picture-book storytelling of a little fisherman and a big fisherman who sail their boats out to sea and catch fish for people in the village. Other titles: *Little Cowboy, Little Fireman.* Very simple. Ages 6-8.

Sneakers. Margaret Wise Brown. Scott. Seven easy-to-read stories about a curious kitten named Sneakers. Charm, humor and warmth. Ages 6-8.

Caps for Sale. Esphyr Slobodkina. Scott. An amusing tale of a peddler, some monkeys and some monkey business. For beginners and older children having a little reading trouble. Ages 6-8.

Up Above and Down Below. Irma E. Webber. Scott. First book about plants for beginners. Ages 6-8.

The Billy and Blaze Books. C. W. Anderson. Macmillan. Five of them mentioned before. Simple text telling real stories. Billy and his horse Blaze have many adventures. Great favorites. Ages 6-8.

900 Buckets of Paint. Edna Becker. Abingdon. An old woman, two cats, donkey and cow set out to find a new home. Picture book, easy to read. Ages 6-8.

Country Train. Jerrold Beim. Morrow. Sam was able to prove that the old country train was able to do something the new train couldn't do. Interesting to little boys. Other titles by same author: *Country Fireman, Country Garage.* Ages 6-8.

The Horse that Takes the Milk Around. Helen Sterling. McKay. Story of the milk horse in rhyme. Ages 6-8.

Little Lost Pigs. Helen Fuller Orton. Lippincott. Real

little pigs that run away and are found by the farm dog. Ages 6-8.

Little Fellow. Marguerite Henry. Winston. The little colt was jealous but finally found happiness. Ages 6-8.

Kitten's Tale. Written and illustrated by Audrey Chalmers. Viking. A little kitten who didn't belong to anyone picked out from the passersby the one she wanted to belong to. *Fancy Be Good* by same author. Ages 6-8.

Sonny Boy Sim. Elizabeth Baker. Rand. What happened one night when the deer and bears were tired of being chased by Sonny Boy and his dog, and turned the tables. Ages 6-8.

Lucky Blacky. Eunice Lackey. Watts. An easy-to-read humorous story of a cat and an old lady. Ages 6-10.

Animal Train. Catherine Woolley. Morrow. Short stories about little animals with repetition that makes them easy to read. Ages 6-10.

Little Auto. Lois Lenski. Oxford. All of the "Mr. Small" books are good for the beginning reader. Children usually know them already by the time they are starting to read, and they get great fun out of reading the stories they have had read to them. Titles: *Little Train, Little Sailboat, Little Airplane, Little Farm, Cowboy Small, Papa Small, etc.*

Surprise for a Cowboy. Clyde Bulla. Crowell. This is an author to remember when you want to buy or borrow books for either your beginning reader or that nine-year-old who hasn't really become a reader yet. There is action in all of Mr. Bulla's stories, and they are extremely easy to read. And they look like real books, not picture books. Danny who had played cowboy at home found out what a real cowboy's life was like. Ages 6-10. Other titles: *Riding the Pony Express, Eagle Feather, A Ranch for Danny, Star of Wild Horse Canyon.*

Dynamite, the Wild Stallion. Nils Hogner. Aladdin Books. How Shorty tamed the wild stallion with patience and kindness. Good for slow readers as well as beginners. Ages 6-10.

The Pottlebys. Gertrude Crampton. Aladdin Books. An easy-to-read book of little stories about a pretty crazy family. *Further Adventures of the Pottlebys.* Ages 6-10.

The Little Old Woman Who Used Her Head. Hope Newell. Nelson. Little stories about the strange old woman who sat and thought. Ages 8-12.

Broomtail. Miriam Mason. Macmillan. A wild proud pony roamed the Western plains until he found a secure life among people. Easy words, large readable print. Useful with older children, too. Ages 8-12. *A Pony Called Lightning,* by same author.

Cloverfield Farm Stories. Helen Fuller Orton. Lippincott. Four smaller books combined into one. Easy-to-read farm stories. Ages 7-10.

Three Boys and a Lighthouse. Nan Agle and Ellen Wilson. Scribner. Three small boys spend an exciting summer on an island lighthouse with their father, the lighthouse keeper. Other titles: *Three Boys and a Tugboat, Three Boys and a Cow.* Ages 7-10.

Cowboy Tommy. Sanford Tousey. Doubleday. One of many by the same author that have been geared for easy reading. *Cowboy Tommy's Roundup, Stagecoach Sam, Val Rides the Oregon Trail.* Ages 7-12.

Suggestions for children having trouble learning to read:

Joan Wanted a Kitty. Jane B. Gemmill. Winston. (See above).

Dynamite, the Wild Stallion. Nils Hogner. Aladdin Books.

Stablemates. Margaret Johnson. Harcourt. An easy-to-read horse story that will interest older children. Ages 8-12. Also *Red Joker, Rolf, an Elkhound of Norway,* and others by same author. There are many titles.

Here Comes Kristie. Written and illustrated by Emma Brock. Knopf. Funny horse story, easy to read, and older children do not mind being seen with it. Other titles: *Kristie and the Colt, Ballet for Mary, Plughorse Derby,* Ages 8-12.

Walt Disney Readers, aforementioned. D. C. Heath. Especially *Mickey Never Never Fails, Donald Duck and His Friends, School Days in Disneyville, Mickey Sees the USA, Donald Duck Sees South America.*

Star of Wild Horse Canyon. Clyde Bulla. Crowell. Described before. Other titles by the same author: *Eagle Feather, A Ranch for Danny, Surprise for a Cowboy, Squanto, Friend of the White Man.*

American Adventure Series. Edited by Emmett Betts. Wheeler Co. This remarkable series lacks literary style but its extreme usefulness in working with children who have trouble learning to read makes up for it. The subject of each of these books is exciting. They are graded so that the first titles in the series are easier. Really invaluable for boy and girl who need reading material that is easy. *Friday the Arapaho Indian, Squanto, Pilot Jack Knight, Buffalo Bill, Davy Crocket, John Paul Jones,* etc. Ask for *The American Adventure Series.* The books are written by different authors.

The True Book Series. Children's Press. As mentioned before, some of these titles are admirably suited for the reader who is having trouble: *Dinosaurs, Policemen and Firemen, Pebbles and Shells, Pets, Science Experiments, Moon, Sun and Stars, Cowboys.*

The First Book Series. Franklin Watts Co. Many of the titles in this enormous series of books about almost everything are simple enough for the nine-year-old who is having reading trouble. *First Book of Cowboys, Indians, Nurses, Baseball.* Almost any of The *First Books* will be useful in helping children read since so often the whole trouble is in finding subjects they are interested in. Pick your subject and find your book in this series. All ages.

Scrambled Eggs Super, and other titles by Dr. Seuss. Random House. Invaluable in creating an interest in reading among those who are having trouble or who don't care to read. *McElligot's Pool, If I Ran the Zoo,* etc. All ages.

Curious George. H. R. Rey. Houghton. This and the other

two titles about George, the monkey, are infallible. All ages love them and can read them.

Street of Little Shops. Margery Bianco. Doubleday. Little stories about little shops in a little town, easy to read for a nine-year-old. *Interesting for all ages.*

Any books of jokes, riddles and funny rhymes are useful for a child who is having difficulty in reading. There are many to choose from. They are suggested under *Funny Books.*

Little Eddie. Written and illustrated by Carolyn Haywood. Morrow. A terribly funny story about a little boy of today who is a born collector, the trouble he gets into and how he comes out on top. Older children do not mind reading this, it is so funny, and it is not hard to read. Other titles equally good: *Eddie and the Fire Engine, Eddie and Gardenia, Eddie's Pay Dirt, Eddie and Big Deals.*

Henry Huggins. Beverly Cleary. Morrow. A small boy gets himself into hilariously funny situations. A little harder to read than *Little Eddie* but definitely not difficult.

B is for Betsy. Written and illustrated by Carolyn Haywood. Harcourt. A little girl and her first year at school. *Betsy and Billy, Betsy and the Boys,* and other titles. All children seem to love these stories, even boys.

When the Mississippi Went Wild. LeGrand. Abingdon. A legend of how Mike Fink tamed the Mississippi. Simple language and interesting illustrations make this a good book for children to read. Other titles: *Why Cowboys Sing in Texas, Cats for Kansas, Tom Benn and Blackbeard the Pirate.* Ages 8-12.

Helen Fuller Orton's Mysteries. Lippincott. Excellent for boys and girls having reading trouble. Ages 8-12.

The Three Policemen. Written and illustrated by William Pene DuBois. Viking. A humorous mystery laid on an island where ordinarily the people are so busy they never do anything wrong. Good for the twelve-year-old, even, who is having trouble reading. *The Great Geppy* by the same author will serve the same purpose. Ages 8-15.

Childhood of Famous Americans. Bobbs. The so-called

"little orange books" by many different authors, about 150 titles in all, about Americans who have made some kind of contribution from historical and literary to other kinds of things. Children are very fond of these. *Older children do not mind reading them even though they are supposed to be for younger children.* The problem is to keep them from reading too many, and keeping children who should be reading something better from reading them. They look so readable, too.

There are many books on science, how-to-do activities that are easy to read. Since children are more interested in reading about something they "cotton" to, there are books on all subjects, if one but hunt, to encourage them to read.

"I get enough reading in school," said the little girl, tossing her head. She was the kind of child who likes to do things, and to sit and listen to grownups talk. Unlike her sister who was scarcely polite because she had her nose in a book, Faith was social. She could read fine. She just preferred to do other things. I once did a very "unprogressive" thing. I offered her ten cents for every book she read, thinking in my "childish ignorance" that it would make her a booklover. I had to part with a dollar and a half. She loved to read no better than before.

There are many children like Faith who just don't care about reading as a pastime. They like to sew, make things in their shops, tinker, play football, and any number of things. But there may be one who just hasn't found the joys of reading, and we should bait him, hoping to make a reader of him, or at least let him know the fun in books.

Here are a few suggestions of bait for those boys and girls. Most of these have been mentioned before.

If I had a boy who didn't like to read I'd buy him:

—if he was a little boy:

Mike Mulligan and His Steam Shovel. Virginia Burton. Houghton.

Flip. Wesley Dennis. Viking.
Curious George. H. R. Rey. Houghton.
Little Toot. Hardi Gramatky. Putnam.
The Little Airplane. Lois Lenski. Oxford.
Jamie and the Dump Truck. Eileen Johnston. Harper.
The Disney Readers. D. C. Heath.

—if he was middle sized:

Mr. Popper's Penguins. Richard and Florence Atwater. Little.
Freddy Goes to Florida. Walter Brooks. Knopf.
Curious George. H. R. Rey. Houghton.
Andy and the Lion. James Daugherty. Viking.
Homer Price. Robert McCloskey. Viking.
Here Comes Kristie. Emma Brock. Knopf.
The Street of Little Shops. Margery Bianco. Doubleday.
Augustus and the River. LeGrand Henderson. Bobbs.
The Mystery in the Old Cave. Helen Fuller Orton. Lippincott.
The Wonder Clock. Howard Pyle. Harper.
Henry Huggins. Beverly Cleary. Morrow.
Otis Spoffard. Beverly Cleary. Morrow
Herbert. Hazel Wilson. Knopf.
Little Eddie. Carolyn Haywood. Morrow.
The Story of Dr. Dolittle. Hugh Lofting. Lippincott.
The Three Policemen. DuBois. Viking.
Miss Pickerell Goes to Mars. Ellen MacGregor. McGraw.

—if he was an older boy:

Ol' Paul. Glen Rounds. Holiday.
Homer Price. Robert McCloskey. Viking.
The Great Geppy. William Pene DuBois. Viking.
Mr. Popper's Penguins. Richard and Florence Atwater. Little.
The Story of Dr. Dolittle. Hugh Lofting. Lippincott.
The Shadow in the Pines. Stephen Meader. Harcourt.
The Kid from Tomkinsville. John R. Tunis. Morrow.

Silver Chief, Dog of the North. Jack O'Brien. Winston.
The Mudhen. Merritt P. Allen. Longmans.

If I had a girl who didn't like to read I'd buy her:

—if she was a little girl:

Billy and Blaze. C. W. Anderson. Macmillan.
Little Lucia. Mabel Robinson.
Fancy Be Good. Audrey Chalmers. Viking.
Flip. Wesley Dennis. Viking.
The Disney Readers. D. C. Heath.
B is for Betsy. Carolyn Haywood. Morrow.

—if she was middle sized:

The Story of Dr. Dolittle. Hugh Lofting. Lippincott.
Little Witch. Anna Bennett. Lippincott.
Ballet for Mary. Emma Brock. Knopf.
Plug Horse Derby. Emma Brock Knopf.
The Saturdays. Elizabeth Enright. Farrar.
Ellen Tebbits. Beverly Cleary. Morrow.
Mr. Popper's Penguins. Richard and Florence Atwater. Little.
The Street of Little Shops. Margery Bianco. Doubleday.
Ginnie and Geneva. Catherine Woolley. Morrow.
Black Stallion. Walter Farley. Random House.
Lassie Come Home. Eric Knight. Winston.
Little House in the Big Woods. Laura I. Wilder. Harper.
The Good Master. Kate Seredy. Viking.

—if she was a big girl:

They Loved to Laugh. Katherine Worth. Doubleday.
Silver Chief, Dog of the North. Jack O'Brien. Winston.
High Hurdles. Frances Duncomb. Sloan.
Watch for a Tall White Sail. Margaret Bell. Morrow.
Seventeenth Summer. Maureen Daly. Dodd.
Candy. Robb White. Doubleday.
Ballet Shoes. Noel Streatfeild. Random House.

XVI

"I have two favorite poems."

POETRY BOOKS

I HAD INVITED the children of the third grade to read me their favorite poems. It was, I admit, a little device to encourage them to read more poetry. The children spent quite a little time during a couple of weeks beforehand looking up poems. The day arrived. We sat in a circle in the library, the children with poetry books with little slips of paper marking their places. I called on Jim. "I have two favorite poems," he said, "one I wrote myself and one by A. A. Milne." How wonderful to be at the age when we don't mind saying that something we ourselves have done is good!

What is poetry? "Poetry is beat and rhythm and dance. It does not walk. It runs, skips, soars, flies," said Stephen Vincent Benét, one of our good American poets.

A poet is trying to tell something. It may be a story, or it may be his own feelings. He is trying to tell it rhythmically in musical words. All poetry needs to be heard as well as read. Poetry is more spontaneous than prose. It sings like music. It makes you feel. The words are vigorous and rich.

Rose Fyleman, the English poet, once asked an audience, "Can anyone tell me what people find in poetry that makes them enjoy it?" There was a moment's silence. Then a little girl in the front row put up a shy hand. "Please, I think it ought to sound pretty." And I suppose, most of all, that is how poetry is different from prose. It "sounds pretty." When prose "sounds pretty" we say it is poetic.

We should try to bring children and poetry together before the children have a chance to grow self-conscious. They get from their elders the feeling that poetry is not interesting. It is sissy. Sometimes children do not like poetry because some adult blundered in selecting a poem to be read. Some poetry is too old for children to understand, the philosophy is too deep, the figures of speech are baffling. Or there are long descriptive passages and inverted sentences. If we wish to interest children in poetry we need to know what they like. They like the singing quality. *Mother Goose Rhymes* have a singing quality. At some periods children like a story in verse. One boy said, "My favorite poem is about the bandit in love with the girl." ("The Highwayman" by Alfred Noyes.) They like poems about feeling, tasting, smelling. Poetry is for the pleasure it gives. It should never be given to children as a reading exercise.

Someone said, "If the children of the world could only become the teachers of adults we might all be taught to be poets, for children have a way of talking in poetry." Children must hear poetry to love it, and once they do love it they will love it forever. So many teachers and parents say they do not like poetry, and surely if they do not like it themselves they cannot make any one else love it.

For little children the picture a poem makes must be obvious: "My bed is a boat." Later the picture can be more subtle.

The person who reads the poems should love them and be able to read them well. He shouldn't avoid words children might not know. Children have an interest in the unknown. When I was about eight years old we learned in school, "The Owl and the Pussy Cat." I recited it to my mother. I came to the phrase "runcible spoon" which I mouthed with delight. My mother was sure I had misunderstood. Such a strange word! But no, there it was in the dictionary.

I had an exciting experience once with children and poetry. I had a manuscript of poetry to try out and I read many poems, to many, many children. Little and big alike, they loved the poems I read. True, they had their favorites. Some liked best the nature poems, and some liked the story poems; many liked the funny ones best. But one and all, they loved the collection.

Said one child, "I think the one who wrote them knows what children think." Said another, "I like the pictures the poems made." And others, "I like the poems because they rhyme and I can see them in my mind." "I loved the words that went into the poems."

If we could remember what poems we liked as children we would probably find that they had to do with things we knew—trees, birds, moon, stars, other children, mother, grandmother, eating, and going to sleep. We would remember the swing of the poem, the rhyme, and certain expressive words. The poet wants to make us see what he sees and feel what he feels. If he does, he has been successful.

Not all children like poetry, but surely every child has some poem he likes, and he might have many more if we grownups knew how to introduce him to them. Poems should be read aloud and shared.

> Oh what a lovely thing
> To see a poem born and made
> And hear it rhyme and sing.*

While we know *Mother Goose Rhymes* are not poetry in the sense of beauty, they are usually the first rhymes a child hears. They are a good introduction to listening to rhythm and rhyme. *Johnny Crow's Garden* is another book of nonsense rhymes for the very young child. And, of course, every child is introduced to *The Night Before Christmas* when he is scarcely able to sit up.

Humorous verses are a good introduction for a child.

* By Barbara Young from *Christopher O.*

Tirra Lirra by Laura E. Richards will amuse the seven-year-old. It is poetry they can understand and laugh at:

Once there was an elephant
Who tried to use the telephant—
No! No! I mean an elephone
Who tried to use the telephone.

Edward Lear's limericks are popular with children a little older.

There was an Old Man of Tobago,
Lived long on rice gruel and sago;
But at last, to his bliss,
The physician said this—
To a roast leg of mutton you may go.

Probably the most satisfactory books for children to have in their own libraries are anthologies of different kinds of poetry. There have been many good ones. And then there should be a few of the individual poets' works that mean most to the individual child.

Favorite Poetry Collections

One Hundred Best Poems for Boys and Girls. Marjorie Barrows. Whitman. A very useful little collection. Ages 8-14.

Under the Tent of the Sky. John Brewton, with drawings by Robert Lawson. Macmillan. Poems about animals, large and small. A very beautiful book. Ages 8-14.

Inheritance of Poetry. Collected and arranged by Gladys Adshead and Anis Duff, with decorations by Nora Unwin. Houghton. All ages.

Sung Under the Silver Umbrella. Poems for younger children. Selected by Literature Committee of the Association for Childhood Education. Illustrated by Dorothy Lathrop. Macmillan. Ages 7-10.

A Rocket in My Pocket. The rhymes and chants of young Americans. Selected by Carl Withers. Holt. A very, very popular collection of amusing rhymes. All ages.

Yours Till Niagra Falls. Lillian Morrison. Rhymes and sayings from autograph volumes. Crowell. Boys and girls of all ages "roar" over this.

The Golden Flute: An anthology of poetry for young children. Edited by Alice Hubbard and Adeline Babbit. Day. This is one of the most useful collections to use with little children, or for older children to use for themselves. The index is by subject, and this is so useful, for with little children very often we want poems on special subjects. Ages 6-10.

Rainbow in the Sky. Edited by Louis Untermeyer. Illustrated by Reginald Birch. Harcourt. (Also his *Singing World for Younger Children*). This covers all the way from lullabies, nonsense verse, seasonal poetry, humorous, animal and birds. Ages 8-12.

A Pocketful of Rhymes. Edited by Katherine Love. Crowell. A charming little volume, nice as a gift for a child. Ages 6-10.

For a Child: Great poems old and new. Edited by Wilma K. McFarland. Westminster. A very beautiful large picture-book-sized book with colored pictures full of detail that interest children very much. The editor was for many years editor of *Child Life Magazine* and knows what children like. Ages 7-10.

Story-Telling Ballads: Selected and arranged for story-telling and reading aloud, and for boys' and girls' own reading. Frances J. Olcott. Houghton. Seventy-seven ballads, narrative poems and Robin Hood Ballads. Ages 10-15.

I Hear America Singing. An anthology of folk poetry edited by Ruth Barnes. Illustrated by Robert Lawson. Winston. Ages 12-16.

The Home Book of Verse for Young Folks. Compiled by Burton K. Stevenson. Decorated by Willy Pogany. Holt. A very complete collection of verse of all kinds. Ages 8-16.

One Thousand Poems for Children. Edited by Elizabeth Sechrist. Based on the selections of Roger Ingpen. Decorative drawings by Henry Pitz. Macrae-Smith. All ages.

Silver Pennies. A collection of modern poems for boys and girls selected by Blanche Jennings Thompson. Illustrated by Winifred Bromhall. Macmillan. One of the cutest and most popular little books imaginable. Ages 8-14.

Some Popular Books of Verse by Individual Poets

A Visit from St. Nicholas ('Twas the Night Before Christmas). Clement C. Moore. One of the most popular and best-known poems. It was in 1822, on Christmas Eve, that Clement Moore, a professor at Columbia, was on his way home with the Christmas turkey. It was dark, snow crunched under his feet, sleighbells were jingling. When he had delivered the package to his wife he shut himself in the study and wrote "A Visit from St. Nicholas" for his grandchildren. It has been delighting children ever since. There are many editions of it. Ages 3-8.

'Twas The Night Before Christmas. Illustrated by Jessie Smith Wilcox. Houghton. One of the oldest editions but still charming.

The Night Before Christmas. Illustrated by Everitt Shinn. Winston.

Night Before Christmas. Illustrated by Leonard Weisgard. Grosset.

The Pied Piper of Hamelin. Robert Browning. Illustrated by Hope Dunlap. Rand. Another masterpiece that has always been popular with children. It was written for a little sick friend. To read it aloud is a real experience. This edition has particularly lovely pictures in soft colors. Ages 8-12.

Everything and Anything. Dorothy Aldis. Putnam. Poems about modern everyday things. Not great poetry but children like it. Good introduction to poetry. Ages 7-9.

Peacock Pie: A Book of Rhymes. Walter De la Mare. Holt. The most popular collection by the great English poet. Ages 8-14.

Poems of Childhood. Eugene Field. Illustrated by Maxfield Parrish. Scribner. A very beautiful volume of the favorites of children for many years. Ages 8-12.

Fairies and Chimneys. Rose Fyleman. Doubleday. This English poet understands fairies. Once when she was lecturing she attempted to recite one of her own poems, but couldn't remember it. A tiny girl on the front row calmly finished it for her. This is one of the favorite collections for children. Ages 9-12.

Complete Book of Nonsense. Edward Lear. Dodd. Lear was called the Father of English Nonsense. His things such as the limericks, "The Owl and the Pussy Cat," "The Jumblies," will live forever. Ages 9-12.

When We Were Very Young and *Now We Are Six.* A. A. Milne. Illustrated by Ernest Shepard. Dutton. These little poems about Christopher Robin are classics today. Rarely is there a child who does not like them. When a youngster is six, or younger, he loves them read to him. When he is ten he reads them again for himself. There are some fine recordings of these poems. Ages 6-12.

Taxis and Toadstools. Rachel Field. Doubleday. Someone said, "She writes through a child's mind and heart." They are about things around a child in city and country. Ages 8-12.

Tirra Lirra. Rhymes old and new. Laura E. Richards. Little. Just out in a new (1955) edition, which means that more children will have a chance to discover this delightful nonsense. Adults will enjoy reading them aloud. Ages 9-14.

Rhymes of Childhood. James Whitcomb Riley. Bobbs. It contains the old favorites. Ages 9-14.

Sing Song. A nursery rhyme book. Christina Rossetti. Macmillan. Beautiful little poems in a lovely little book. Ages 6-10.

A Child's Garden of Verses. Robert Louis Stevenson. There are many editions of these most favorite poems. Stevenson seemed to get right into the feelings of a child. One edition illustrated by Jessie Wilcox Smith. Scribner's is a large, beautiful edition. Ages 4-10. Another is illustrated by Roger Duvoisin. Heritage Press. A lovely book. A tiny one, illustrated with the dainty drawings of Tasha Tudor, is published by Oxford. It is possible to buy one from fifty cents up. Every child should have his *Garden of Verses* so he will grow up knowing them.

Little Whistler. Frances Frost. Illustrated by Roger Duvoisin. Whittlesey House. A great favorite with children. The poet is one of our best living American poets. Ages 7-10.

Summer Green. Elizabeth Coatsworth. Illustrated by Nora Unwin. Macmillan. Beautiful poems that children will appreciate, by one of our best poets. A new collection by the same poet, perfectly delightful, is about mice and called *Mouse Chorus.* Pantheon.

Poems for Youth. Emily Dickinson. Little. A selection by Alfred L. Hampson. Poems especially appreciated by young people. Ages 12-16.

Johnny Appleseed, and Other Poems. Vachel Lindsay. Macmillan. Every child should know Vachel Lindsay's poems. This is a good introduction. Ages 9-14.

Poems Selected for Young People. Edna St. Vincent Millay. Harper. Ages 10-16.

Early Moon. Carl Sandburg. Illustrated by James Daugherty. Harcourt. Not all of Sandburg's poetry do children understand, but this will be a good introduction to a poet whose name they should know. Ages 10-16.

Stars Tonight. Sara Teasdale. Illustrated by Dorothy Lathrop. Macmillan. Poems about nature. Ages 10-16.

Book of Americans. Rosemary and Stephen Benét. Rinehart. Fifty-six poems describing the life and character of famous American men and women from Columbus to Woodrow Wilson. Most of them have a humorous tinge. My two favorites are "Nancy Hanks" and "Abraham Lincoln." For all ages. Good for family reading.

Many children think poets are dead. It is up to us old folks to prove to them that poetry is alive.

XV

"My father says to get a classic."

THE CLASSICS

I DON'T KNOW how many times through the years a child has said to me, "My father (or mother, or grandmother) says to get a classic." Sometimes it has annoyed me very much because the child has needed just good reading to make her equal to the classics. And once I remember retorting, a bit impertinently, I am afraid, "Ask your father what a classic is."

What is a classic? I consulted a dictionary. It says something like this: "A literary or art work of acknowledged excellence." It doesn't say that it has to be fifteenth century, eighteenth century, or even old. Of course, the fact that a book is still in print, still read by some people, is pretty sure proof that it is good, or at least has been liked by a lot of people through the ages. On the other hand, just as with many things that we accept without question because we have not stopped to reconsider, some of the classics have lost their usefulness, but because once we considered them good we have kept right on thinking so.

What the father mentioned above would have suggested for his little girl I have no way of knowing, but I'll bet he would have been stumped. The trouble with us old ones in regard to children's classics is that we left off being children a long time ago, and for us the classics ended then. The fact that twenty or thirty or forty years have passed and newer books have begun to become classics does not enter our heads. We still think in terms of *Hans Brinker, or The Silver Skates* and *Toby Tyler.*

How long does it take to make a classic? As Josette Frank says in her admirable book, *Your Child's Reading Today,* some books may just be long-lived, not classic. That may prove true of many of the books today that are of "acknowledged excellence"; but some of them surely will be in the top ranks for generations, and are far better than some of those we so fondly cherish in our remembrance.

Of course we want our children to read the good old books that have meant so much to so many generations. They have much to offer that modern books do not seem to have. The old books give continuity to our lives, books that have run through several generations and are known by grandparents, parents and children. They have beauty in words and feeling. They are long and leisurely, with a chance to develop character and plot. They are, as has been said before, like a common language that we who know them understand. They have a universal quality.

I once announced that all library books had to be returned by the Wednesday before school closed. Betty responded, "Now don't beef, Miss Fenner. I'm not returning my books until Friday. Grandma's reading them." Yes, good books are universal.

We folks who love the classics also know that with the years the memory of them, what they meant, their people so real to us, the wisdom of them, grows deeper. As May Lamberton Becker wrote in her book *Adventures in Reading,* speaking of the classics, "The older one gets the more one sees in them. It is like climbing a hill, the scene is the same but we get a different perspective." And as J. Donald Adams wrote in The New York *Times* about *The Wind in the Willows,* which is surely classic in dimension, in regard to Mole's coming home and his pleasure at being there again, "It is the truth that every adventurer comes to know. It is the same impulse that, in reading, brings us back from time to time to the old tried favorites, the books which we know will never let us down. To recognize and accept the strength of that desire is not to shut the door against new experiences, whether in the world or in books; it is merely to leave the door open, both for departure and return."

It is not to be wondered at that we want our children to enjoy what we remember *we* read (or intended to) and enjoyed. What we forget is the change in times, for time has rushed along these last thirty years. Times have changed not only for adults but for children as well. Things are telescoped, hurried, speeded up. While we lament that it is so, and always think that sometime we will be leisurely again, I suspect that that time will never come because we have established a rhythm of living. Children and adults alike want their stories fast-moving, with action at the very beginning, not too many descriptive passages, a compact story.

I remember hearing Hugh Walpole tell a story about Thackeray. *Vanity Fair* was being printed in a magazine serially as Mr. Thackerey wrote it, and even he didn't know how it was coming out. A reader wrote him saying, "Dear Mr. Thackeray, I am getting tired of Becky Sharp. Won't you please write about someone else for a change?" And being an obliging man, the author did write about someone else for the next few installments. Someone asked Mr. Thackeray how he kept track of so many characters. He replied, "I put them in and then just run along behind them to hear what they are talking about."

The classics are melodramatic, often sentimental, sad. Nowadays authors are almost afraid to make their stories sad, even though children are noted for loving sad tales, because parents don't want their children to face the facts of life. No modern book for children would have a death like Little Nell's.

If we want our children to read the old books, timing is

very important. We give our children things before they are ready for them, so eager are we to have them get the things we love. The electric train father gives son for Christmas is not appreciated until years later. Father plays with it. In the same way, we often give books to children before they are ready. Donald's aunt wanted so for him to love books that she began building up a library for him the minute he started in school. What did she buy? The classics, of course, in nice bindings. Donald not only could not appreciate them then, but he was slow in learning to read. Had she given him *Little Eddie* it would have been better. He would have been more interested and would have learned to read by reading. How often we hear people say, "I think I must have read that book when I was too young to understand it." And so often the books we had before we were ready we never go back to; we only remember that we thought them dull because we did not understand. Even if we could read the words they meant little. We did not "get" the thing that has made the book live all these years.

When an older person goes to a book shop, and he has not kept up on what is new and good, he looks around. A familiar title catches his eye. (How we love and feel secure with familiar things!) He doesn't recognize *The Moffats,* or *Homer Price,* or even *Mary Poppins.* His eye lights on *Heidi.* He has heard of it (so has the clerk). And doesn't it say on the bottom of the back strip "Children's Classics"? It must be good. It is likely to be in a more attractive edition at a lower price than new books, partly because it is royalty-free. He buys it. It may be entirely too old or for the wrong person.

To encourage children to read these books we must have enthusiasm. We can't force them on them. Just by saying "Bring home a classic" we will not make our children enjoy it. If we are truly infatuated with Dickens and Scott or Charles Kingsley and Lewis Carroll, then we will have patience to approach our children in the right way. We will naturally be enthusiastic. Does a father say to his son "You must like baseball?" No, he talks it, takes him to baseball games, pitches a ball to him now and then, instructs him how to hold his bat. If we value the classics, we must spend intelligence, time, imagination in encouraging our children to read them.

Don't say "Get *Tom Sawyer* from the library and read it." That is, don't if you're smart. Begin with your love of it, with recollections of some of the amusing things you enjoyed. When the book comes home with the boy, take a little time out, look at it, read some of it to him to start him off. See that the edition has good type and spacing and illustrations. The chances are the edition you were brought up with, and even may have in your library, is dull-looking. Remember, you are competing with hundreds of good new books of his own period. Even thirty years ago when we were younger, there was not the competition there is today.

A mother told me she was reading *Hans Brinker or the Silver Skates* aloud to her youngster. She made a wry face; "It seems rather dull," she said. We ourselves cannot always tell when a thing is dated. I read *Princess and the Goblins* aloud to a group of nine-year-olds. I was quite conscious of the unusual sentence structure and words and the "talking down." The children adored it. It had no date as far as they were concerned. Some books don't have the story appeal to carry them beyond the datedness.

A word should be said about abridged and adapted versions of the classics. The theory is that a young person might better read *Lorna Doone* cut and simplified, than not to read it at all. The opposite side says a child might better miss the story than not to have it the way the author wrote it. The answer, I think, is in how good the abridgment is, and of what book. *The Three Musketeers,* so far as I know, is always "abridged" for young people. Chapters have been removed without influencing the story whatsoever. But where a book has been entirely rewritten for youngsters I would be suspicious. Is it necessary for a child to read *Robinson Crusoe* before he is really old enough? Can't he wait? He has the rest of his life for an adult story like that. The fact that a child does like the main, exciting part of the story, the shipwreck, does not mean he has to read it when he is eight. A young mother told me she had read *Huckleberry Finn* to her small daughter. But she added, "I admit I changed some of the words because I didn't want Mary to hear them." The mother should have waited for her daughter to grow old enough to read Mark Twain's words. If you are eager to have your children know *Treasure Island* or *Tom Sawyer,* read them aloud. They will love them. Later they will read them to themselves.

We have some books coming out each year that we speak of as "new" classics because we are sure they will be long-lived. They have already been tested by the children, reviewed favorably by the adults. Some, if times change as rapidly in the next thirty years as they have in the past thirty, will later become out of date. Time alone will tell.

Below is a list of some of the classics old and new that children really read and enjoy. But remember . . . it is important to get *the right book at the right time.* Build a background for your child's appreciation, and by all means enter into it with enthusiasm and patience.

"What a sense of security in an old book that Time has criticized for us."

Classics for the Youngest

Johnny Crow's Garden. Written and illustrated by Leslie Brooke. Warne. A classic picture book with nonsense rhymes. Ages 2-5.

The Tale of Peter Rabbit. Written and illustrated by Beatrix Potter. Warne. A necessity for every child to have in its original edition.

A little boy was trying to tell his mother what the Sunday School lesson was about. He began, "Peter said to Jesus," and he then couldn't remember. Later he tried again but got no further. Finally he said, "Well, what would a rabbit say?" Peter to children is Peter Rabbit. Ages 2-6.

The Story of Little Black Sambo. Written and illustrated by Helen Bannerman. Lippincott. In spite of the controversy about it, it is one of the favorite books with children. They love to "play" it and hear it again and again. Ages 4-6.

Pelle's New Suit. Written and illustrated by Elsa Beskow. Harper. Lovely pictures tell how Pelle earned his new suit by raking hay, bringing in wood, feeding pigs, going errands. Swedish. Ages 5-7.

Some that are well on their way to being classics

A B C Bunny. Written and illustrated by Wanda Gag. Coward. Beautiful lithographs showing the bunny hopping from A to Z. Ages 1-5.

Millions of Cats. Written and illustrated by Wanda Gag. Coward. Bound to be demanded by children for generations to come. Ages 4-7.

The Story About Ping. Marjorie Flack. Illustrated by Kurt Wiese. A favorite story with the 5-7-year-olds.

Mike Mulligan and His Steam Shovel. Written and illustrated by Virginia Burton. Houghton. Mike and Mary Ann are favorites. Ages 4-8.

Five Chinese Brothers. Claire Huchet Bishop. Illustrated by Kurt Wiese. Coward. Forever popular with young and old. Ages 5-10.

Andy and the Lion. Written and illustrated by James Daugherty. Viking. An old story retold with vigorous illustrations. Ages 6-10.

Tried and true for the slightly older child

Grimm's Fairy Tales. Many editions. All the old favorites are here. Ages 8-12.

Andersen's Fairy Tales. Many editions. Ages 10-12.

The Princess and the Goblins. George Macdonald. Illustrated by Nora Unwin. Macmillan. *The Princess and Curdie,* the miner's son, overcome the wicked goblins. Ages 9-12.

Heidi. Johanna Sypri. Illustrated by Agnes Tait. Lippincott. Most children adore this old story. Ages 9-12. It is full of Heidi's fondness for her grandfather, her Swiss mountain home and her goats. There is both humor and sadness in it that finds a response with children.

The Adventures of Pinocchio. C. Collodi (pseud). Illustrated after Attilio Mussino. Macmillan. An Italian classic for children. The pranks and adventures of a wooden marionette. Ages 9-12.

Bambi. Felix Salten. Noble. The life story of a fawn poetically told. Ages 10-15.

Black Beauty. Anna Sewell. Many editions. People can say until Doomsday that this is a sentimental story full of moralizing but children still vote it their favorite book. Ages 8-12.

The Bird's Christmas Carol. Kate Douglas Wiggin. Illustrated by Jessie Gillespie. Houghton. Children love the sentimentality and humor in this story of the rich little girl who invited the poor Ruggleses for Christmas dinner. Ages 8-12.

The Magic Fishbone. Crarles Dickens. Illustrated by Louis Slobodkin. Vanguard. The trials and rewards of the Princess Alicia in taking care of her eighteen brothers and sisters. Ages 9-12.

The Wind in the Willows. Kenneth Grahame. Illustrated by Ernest Shepard. Scribner. Many other editions too. "One does not argue about *The Wind in the Willows.* The young man gives it to the girl with whom he is in love, and if she does not like it, asks her to return his letters. The older man tries it on his nephew, and alters his will accordingly. The book is a test of character. We can't criticize it because it is criticizing us. When you sit down to it, don't be so ridiculous as to suppose that you are sitting in judgment on my taste, or on the art of Kenneth Grahame. You are merely sitting in judgment on yourself. You may be worthy: I don't know. But it is you who are on trial." Thus wrote A. A. Milne in his introduction to the Heritage Press edition. It is a book you love. It becomes an enduring possession, and you reread it all your life. Ages 10 and up.

The Just So Stories. Rudyard Kipling. Illustrated by Rajankovsky. Doubleday. The most famous stories: "Elephant's Child," "How the Leopard Got His Spots," "How the Rhinoceros Got His Skin," "How the Camel Got His Hump." These are in separate volumes also. Children should have these read to them. The language is perfect. Ages 6-10.

Alice's Adventures in Wonderland. Lewis Carroll. Illustrated by John Tenniel. Macmillan. Many other editions. Not all children like this. Some will like it younger than others. Worth trying, and later coming back to it. It is said that Ethel Barrymore reads it every year to help her imagination. 9 to any age.

The Swiss Family Robinson. Johann D. Wyss. Illustrated by Harry Roundtree. Macmillan. Many other editions. Children love this improbable tale. A Swiss family shipwrecked on a desert island find many incongruous things that children accept. And as someone said, "Why shouldn't they?" Nothing is impossible to children. Ages 8-12.

Treasure Island. Robert Louis Stevenson. Illustrated by N. C. Wyeth. Scribner. One of the best-loved stories. Quite young children love it read aloud. As one youngster said so wisely, "Stevenson made it a point to be exciting." Ages 9-15.

The Adventures of Tom Sawyer. Mark Twain. Harper. One of the most popular books of all times. Ages 10-14.

The Adventures of Huckleberry Finn. Mark Twain. Harper. Someone was asked what American book would be alive in two hundred years. The reply was *Huckleberry Finn.* Ages 12-16.

Twenty Thousand Leagues Under the Sea. Jules Verne. Illustrated by N. C. Wyeth. Scribner. Unfortunately because of the movie many children too young for it are wanting to read this story of Captain Nemo and his submarine. Boys and girls of 12 and up will find it an absorbing tale.

Mysterious Island is another popular story by the same author.

Little Women. Louisa May Alcott. The story of Meg, Jo,

Beth and Amy. Illustrated by Jessie Wilcox Smith. Little. Many men writers have given this book credit for influencing them. When the first movie of it came out, many boys read it with *brown paper covers over the title.* Girls still enjoy it. It is amazingly fresh and undated. Ages 10-15.

Robinson Crusoe. Daniel Defoe. Illustrated by E. Boyd Smith. Houghton. Many editions. A great story. Children especially like the saving of the things from the wreck, the building of his house, and the daily scrabbling for a living. The beginning of the book is hard going and has been taken out from some editions. Every child should know this book but there is no hurry. Ages 12-16.

Rip Van Winkle and the Legend of Sleepy Hollow. Washington Irving. Illustrated by Maude and Miska Petersham. Macmillan. Not easy to read but children enjoy having it read to them. Ages 10-15.

The Jungle Book. Rudyard Kipling. Illustrated by Kurt Wiese. Doubleday. Especially should children know the Mowgli stories and "Rikki Tikki Tavi." Ages 8-14.

The Merry Adventures of Robin Hood. Written and illustrated by Howard Pyle. Scribner. The very finest edition of the Robin Hood stories; belongs in every teen-age boy's library. Ages 10-15.

The Story of King Arthur and His Knights. Written and illustrated by Howard Pyle. Scribner. The finest King Arthur. Not easy to read but a book to own for the rest of your life. Ages 12-16.

The Three Musketeers. Alexandre Dumas. Illustrated. Dodd. A favorite with children in their teens. Swashbuckling and exciting. Ages 14-18.

The Count of Monte Cristo. Alexandre Dumas. Illustrated by Mead Schaeffer. Dodd. I have known boys who had read this tale of revenge many times. A dramatic story for all time. Ages 14-18.

The Peterkin Papers. Lucretia Hale. Illustrated by Harold

Brett. Houghton. One of the funniest books that will be enjoyed by the whole family. Ages 10 and up.

Some more recent books that no doubt will make the "classic" list.

Winnie the Pooh. A. A. Milne. Illustrated by Ernest Shepard. Dutton. Story of Christopher Robin and his teddy bear. Ages 8-10.

The Story of Doctor Dolittle. Written and illustrated by Hugh Lofting. Lippincott. An unusual Doctor who knows the language of animals goes to Africa to vaccinate the monkeys and is given an animal called a pushmipullyu as his reward. Wonderful. Ages 7-10.

Mary Poppins. P. L. Travers. Illustrated by Mary Shepard. Reynal. A story of the remarkable things that happened after Mary Poppins arrived on an east wind to look after the Banks children. Delightful nonsense that children from 6 to 12 love.

Homer Price. Written and illustrated by Robert McCloskey. Viking. Six stories about that unusual boy, Homer. Not difficult to read, and loved by all children. Ages 7-12.

The Street of Little Shops. Margery Bianco. Illustrated by Grace Paull. Doubleday. Little stories about little shops in a little town. Children find them delightful and easy to read. Ages 7-10.

The Moffats. Eleanor Estes. Illustrated by Louis Slobodkin. Harcourt. A charming family story with four interesting children, but especially Jane and Rufus. Ages 10-14.

Mr. Popper's Penguins. Richard and Florence Atwater. Illustrated by Robert Lawson. Little. The amusing adventures of the Poppers and their penguins. Ages 7-12.

Rabbit Hill. Written and illustrated by Robert Lawson. Viking. The little animals watch anxiously for the new people who move into the house on the hill. They find them most considerate. A beautiful story with lovely pictures. Ages 6-12.

The Little House in the Big Woods, and others of same

series. Laura Ingalls Wilder. Illustrated by Garth Williams. Harper. These stories by their very reality will live for a long long time. The children know the characters so well. Ages 8-14.

Call It Courage. Written and illustrated by Armstrong Sperry. Macmillan. A great story of a Polynesian boy who sets out to prove his courage and goes through terrific adventures. Children love it best when it is read to them. Ages 10-14.

The Wonder Clock and *Pepper and Salt.* Written and illustrated by Howard Pyle. Harper. Stories based on old folk tale plots. Wonderful for the story hour and for children to read for themselves. Ages 8-12.

Men of Iron. Written and illustrated by Howard Pyle. Harper. A terrific story of the training of a knight in the Middle Ages. Beautifully written. Ages 12-16.

The Dark Frigate. Charles Hawes. Illustrated by A. O. Fischer. Little. The story of Philip Marsham who lived in time of King Charles. An excellent sea story. Ages 13-16. As one boy said of it, "If you like suspense, adventure, and pirates, I recommend this book."

Caddie Woodlawn. Carol Ryrie Brink. Illustrated by Kate Seredy. Macmillan. A story of Wisconsin in the early days and a girl who was allowed to be a tomboy. Her adventures are both exciting and humorous. Ages 10-14. "Every girl from nine to ninety would enjoy it," wrote Missy.

The Good Master. Written and illustrated by Kate Seredy. Viking. The kind of book that is read and reread. How can it help but become a classic? Kate and her cousin Jansci have many adventures on the Hungarian Plains. Ages 8-14.

Ship's Parrot. Honoré Morrow and William Swartzman. Illustrated by Gordon Grant. Morrow. A lovely story of a boy who takes his parrot to sea. The parrot helps solve a mystery. Ages 8-10.

Jim Davis. John Masefield. Lippincott. A tale of smugglers on the English coast. Ages 10-14.

XVI

"I could listen to stories the rest of my life."

STORIES TO READ AND TELL

I HAD BEEN TELLING stories at Lake George. At the end, a little girl sat looking dreamily into the distance. "I could listen to stories the rest of my life," she said. "You'd wanta eat, wouldn't yuh?" said a little boy. Men were ever thus!

Yes, children could listen to good stories for the rest of their lives. Even the busy fellows who won't take time away from their inventions to read to themselves like to be read to. Whether a story is told or read, if it is a good story, a story worthy to be shared, the children like it. Their shining faces, sometimes thoughtful, or, like the little girl's, dreamy, their ejaculations at the end, are reward enough for any parent or teacher. Even their interruptions prove their interest. I was telling "Clever Peter and the Two Bottles" to a group of seven-year-olds. It begins, "Yes, Peter was clever. His mother said so." John interrupted me, "My grandmother says I'm a genius." If we would tell stories and read to children, we have to learn that there will be occasional interruptions. When a very little child says, "Oh, I know that one," he is complimenting you, not being critical. He likes to be in the know. It doesn't mean he doesn't want to listen.

I was going to tell stories to my six-year-old nephew at bedtime. He said, "Now don't tell me 'The Jackal and the Alligator.' You've told it before. As a matter of fact, I've told it to quite a few kids myself." And *that* was a compliment, to have my story repeated to others.

One of my earliest and loveliest recollections is of my mother's telling me stories. I don't remember that she ever read to me but she must have had a great fund of fairy tales—the old favorites, "The Three Bears," "Henny Penny," "The Three Little Pigs," I have only to halt a minute to remember how her voice sounded as she said, "I swear by the hairs of my chinny chin chin." Her "Fee, fi, fo, fum" in "Jack and the Bean Stalk" made glorious chills run up and down my spine. My favorite of all, however, was "The Little Red Hen." That little hen was a real personality to me. What those stories meant to me, being told as my mother was busy sewing, cannot be measured. It meant a wealth of background of old tales, a love of them which has persisted, and a love of storytelling. Too, it meant a close communication with my mother, and we had a sort of common language built on those old tales. Once, and this was when I was grown up, there was chicken left from the meal before, too little to serve the family. Helping mother prepare the meal I saw the plate of chicken in the kitchen. During the meal mother got up for something. When she returned she looked at me significantly and said, "Top off." I knew well what she meant from the story, "A Cat and Mouse in Partnership" that she had told me years before. She had been "nipping" at the chicken.

Reading aloud to children is one of the most rewarding of all activities. It not only introduces them to books they should have before they are able to read to themselves, things like "Millions of Cats," "Angus and the Ducks," "The Just So Stories." It also trains them to be good listeners. After all, listening is a habit. Telling stories to a group of children from a small "progressive" school one time was one of the most frustrating jobs I ever did. Not one of those children had ever been taught to listen. The habit of listening pays all one's life. Too few people, small or large, have it. What is that definition of a bore? "A person who talks about himself while you want to talk about yourself." There would be fewer bores in the world if people not only were trained to listen to someone else, but also, as a result of reading and listening, had something interesting to say.

Reading aloud is a family experience. It is easy to tell, in working with children, the ones who have been read to and the ones who haven't.

Reading to younger children has come to be more or less an accepted thing, but reading to older children or to a family group is done less today with all the other attractions taking the time. Reading to a group provides a unity, a cohesion, that is wonderful. It is common bond of interest. It brings up plenty of things for family talk and discussion. A child who has been read to shows results in his speech and wider experience with languages. And definitely, if the reading is of good books, it is the beginning of good taste in literature.

One mother told me that each night she and her son and daughter took turns reading. It was especially good for the youngest, who needed reading practice.

There are some suggestions I would make, and things I would avoid in reading or telling stories to children.

Don't change the words in a story. A friend of mine told me he had been reading "The Three Billy Goats Gruff" to his four-year-old boy. He said, "Of course, we don't say 'troll' to Tommy because he wouldn't know what a troll was. We say 'bear.' " "What is a troll?" I asked my friend. He looked a little startled. Tommy knew more about trolls than his father did. Children's imaginations picture things. No one knows what a troll looks like. After all, he is an imaginary creature. Why change it to "bear" for a child any more than for an adult? A child loves imaginary things.

Another friend told me that in reading "Little Auto" she

said "car" instead of auto. "Jimmy doesn't know 'auto,' " she explained. What a chance to teach Jimmy what auto was! Children are brighter than even their parents think.

A family I know did a great deal of reading together. Sunday nights the father read aloud to the whole group. It was a wonderful thing to do, and I appreciated that fact, *but* there were some things I couldn't bear to have him read to them because he spoiled them forever and all time. *The Wind in the Willows* was taken home to be read. I inquired from one of the children how they were liking it, and the youngest said, "Daddy stops all the time to see if we know what the words mean." I was there for dinner a short time afterwards, and he himself brought up the subject of the difficult words in the book. I remarked that I thought it was good for children to hear big words. From the rest of the context they would get the meaning, and learn many new words. He looked at me strangely and said, "That is a new idea." Anyway, I made a pretext of needing the book and got it away from him before he ruined it for the children.

In selecting something to read to children, choose something a bit beyond their own reading ability, something to stretch them. Children's interests run ahead of their reading ability. Children can "take" much more than we think. Especially if reading to a family group or any group of assorted ages, aim at the oldest. It is surprising what the youngest get. If you aim at the youngest, the oldest ones are bored. I used to tell "Billy Beg and His Bull" to ten-year-olds, never below that age for I thought it wouldn't interest younger children, and was too long. Then one day, to break up a long story hour, I asked some first graders if they had any stories to tell me. A six-year-old boy not only proceeded to tell "Billy Beg" but he told it with many of the words from the original story. I was amazed, and asked where he had heard the story. "You told it to the sixth grade. My brother is in it. He told it to me." After that I wasn't so afraid of what the little fellows could understand.

Children will enjoy poetry read aloud. After all, poetry needs to be read aloud—Lear's *Complete Nonsense Book,* Richard's *Tirra Lirra,* story poems such as "Paul Revere's Ride." One of the nicest books to read to a group is *The Book of Americans* by the Benéts.

There is one problem, a small problem if parents do not worry too much about it. The child who has been read to a great deal may be slower in beginning to read to himself. We shouldn't be alarmed since it is only natural that it should be so. What is read to him is so much more exciting and interesting than what he can read to himself for a long time. His pre-primers are pretty slow compared to stories with real plots. I remember Stephen who had had really big books read to him when he was quite little. When he started in school he had trouble in his reading. Once when I was at his house he wanted to show me that he could read. We sat on a sofa together with his pre-primer. He read painfully to me something like this: "John played. Jane played. Jip played. John and Jane played with Jip." Stephen was embarrassed. He looked up at me. "You see, it means they really played," he said. Children should be given chances to read to themselves and to us, too, in addition to being read to. What a wealth of background they will grow up with from the books read to them! What a bond a family has that enjoys things together!

Children like the same stories over and over and over. A friend of mine has learned "Snow White and the Seven Dwarfs" practically by heart, she has had to read it aloud so often. I guess the children know it by heart too, but they want nothing else. There will come a time when, subtly maybe, she will slip in something else.

The reading-aloud time should be relaxing. It is fun to have a regular time for reading but to force it when it is not timely spoils the fun, too. And the length of the reading time depends on the interest shown. Some children can sit still longer than others. Judging by the amusing account by

John Mason Brown of his attempts to get his family together to read, one should not choose a time when there is a radio program the children want to listen to. As I remember it, one after another of the group made an excuse to get away, leaving Mr. Brown reading *Treasure Island* to himself by the fire.

There is nothing more fun than *telling* stories . . . if you like it. Children love to listen to a storyteller. "I like her stories best," said the boy of one storyteller. "She's got hers in her head." There is no book between the storyteller and her audience. Eyes meet, attention is there, especially with a group. The old folk tales are good for telling because they were told in the first place. They have simple straightforward plots, something happening all the time, a definite pattern, if you will notice, that makes them easy to remember. There are some collections of stories that are very useful to a storyteller.

Books for Storytelling

Mighty Mikko. Parker Fillmore. Harcourt. A collection of Finnish folk tales. Another of his, Czechoslovakian tales: *The Shoemaker's Apron* (especially good for little children) and *Czechoslovakian Fairy Tales.* Ages 7-12.

Tales from Grimm. Written and illustrated by Wanda Gag. Coward. The best telling of Grimm for little children. They sound as if they were being told as you read them. Ages 6-10.

Time to Laugh. Stories selected by Phyllis Fenner. Illustrated by Henry Pitz. Knopf. A collection of funny stories from folk lore and modern fantasy that children enjoy very much. Ages 8-12. Another by the same author has old favorites and many other tales: *Giants and Witches and a Dragon or Two, Adventure, Rare and Magical.* Stories very popular with children. Ages 8-12.

Told Under the Blue Umbrella. Association for Childhood Education. Macmillan. Collection of stories for little children. Ages 4-8.

Favorite Stories Old and New. Collected by Sidonie Gruenberg. Illustrated by Kurt Wiese. Doubleday. All kinds of stories are represented here, a big collection. Ages 4-10.

Read-To-Me Story Book. Child Study Association, and *Read Me Another Story,* by the same. Crowell. An excellent collection of many *first* stories. Ages 4-10.

There are some books that just cry out to be read aloud, and many of them would not be known to children if they did not hear them read. They can enjoy them and understand them long before they could read them to themselves.

Books that need to be read aloud

(Of course, this list will not include all the fine picture books that naturally are read to children.)

The Just So Stories. Rudyard Kipling. Doubleday. Illustrated by Rojankovsky. Other editions, too. These nonsense stories about the origin of the elephant's trunk, the camel's hump, the Rhinoceros's skin, and so on, should be a part of every child's background. They need to be read to children because they will enjoy them when they are quite little. The language is unique and charming and should never be changed. Ages 6-10.

Poppy Seed Cakes. Mary E. Clark and Margery Quigley. Doubleday. Four-year-old Andrewshek and little Erminka came from the old country with old aunt Katushka. Gay little stories with a quaint touch. Little children love them. Ages 6-9.

A Street of Little Shops. Margery Bianco. Illustrated by Grace Paull. Doubleday. A little story about each of the shops in a little town. "Mr. A. and Mr. P." is a great favorite with little children. When children are eight or nine they read it to themselves. They never seem to tire of it. I can't tell you the charm of these little stories. They are the kind some grownups look at and say, "Children wouldn't like these. Nothing much happens." But children *do* enjoy them. Ages 7-12.

Mary Poppins. P. L. Travers. Illustrated by Mary Shepard. Harcourt. This astonishing nursemaid blew in on an east wind and stayed until the wind changed. Many remarkable things occurred while she was there. There is no age at which a child does not enjoy this book. I have known four-year-olds to demand it again and again. And many ten-year-olds are still enjoying it. Parents will enjoy it too. Ages 6-12.

April's Kittens. Written and illustrated by Claire Newberry. Harper. The complications that arose when April's cat, Sheba, had three kittens in what her father called a "one-cat apartment." Quite little children, pre-school, love this story. Others equally good are *Marshmallow, Mittens, T Bone the Baby Sitter*. Ages 6-10.

The Story of Babar. Written and illustrated by Jean deBrunhoff. Translated from the French by Merle Haas. Random. Babar, the little elephant, ran away from the jungle and went to live with an old lady in Paris. Gay and amusing. The story is written in script which children cannot read for themselves for a long time. Ages 4-8.

The Five Hundred Hats of Bartholomew Cubbins. Written and illustrated by Dr. Seuss. Bartholomew never suspected there was anything strange about his hat until the day he took it off to the king. Each time he took it off there was another hat to take its place. No one could solve the mystery. Ages 6-10.

And to Think That I Saw It on Mulberry Street. Written and illustrated by Dr. Seuss. Vanguard. A nonsense story in verse of the things that went on in a small boy's mind when he saw a plain horse and cart on Mulberry Street. Ages 6-10.

Miss Hickory. Carolyn Sherwin Bailey. With lithographs by Ruth Gannett. Viking. Miss Hickory was a countrywoman with a hickory-nut head and an apple-tree twig for a body. This is a story of how she and her unusual neighbors survived when her little-girl owner left for the winter. A very beautiful story appreciated by six-year-olds, and up. Should be read by an enthusiastic adult. Ages 7-12.

Charlotte's Web. E. B. White. Pictures by Garth Williams.

Harper. The story of a little girl who could talk to animals, but especially the story of Wilbur, the pig, and his friendship with Charlotte, the spider who could not only talk but write as well. This will interest the adult reader as well as the child. All ages. *Stuart Little* by the same author is also popular.

Ragman of Paris and His Ragamuffins. Told and illustrated by Elizabeth Orton Jones. Oxford. Charming little stories about Mich and Toby and the Ragman of Paris, and other interesting characters. Quite little children will love these stories. Ages 5-8.

Tag-along Tooloo. Frances Clarke Sayers. Illustrated by Helen Sewell. Viking. Five-year-old Tallulah was a nuisance because she wanted to tag along after her sister. When she couldn't she got into mischief. Little children love these little stories. Ages 6-8. *Sally Tait* by the same author is for slightly older children.

Mère Michel and Her Cat. Margaret Cardew. Day. A "classic" translated from the French. A delightful and hilarious story of a stray cat adopted by the Countess, and his struggle to live because of his enemies. He had not nine, but many lives, apparently. Children adore this story, as do adults who read it to them. A lovely-looking little book, too. Ages 7-12.

Rabbit Hill. Written and illustrated by Robert Lawson. Viking. The animals on Rabbit Hill in Connecticut are very excited when they learn that new folks are coming to live in the Big House. A charming story of country life. Children enjoy it most when it is read aloud. Lovely things are much more fun when shared. To be fully appreciated even by an adult it really must be read aloud. A sequel, *Tough Winter,* is just as beautiful as *Rabbit Hill.* The illustrations of these books are simply gorgeous. Both are books to own and books to treasure. All ages.

Little Blacknose. Hildegarde Hoyt Swift. Illustrated by Llynd Ward. Harcourt. The story of the DeWitt Clinton engine that stands on the balcony at Grand Central Station, and particularly of the memorable day when he made history by drawing the first train from Albany to Schenectady. Ages 7-10.

Winnie the Pooh. A. A. Milne. Illustrated by Ernest Shepard. Dutton. The story of Christopher Robin and his Teddy Bear. The characters of this modern classic are as real to the children as their next-door neighbors. All ages.

Floating Island. Written and illustrated by Anne Parrish. Harper. The strange adventures of Mr. and Mrs. Doll and their three children when shipwrecked on the shore of a tropical island. Both boys and girls delight in this story when it is read to them. Ages 7-12.

The Treasure Seekers. Edith Bland (E. Nesbit). Coward. An attempt by the Bastable children to recoup the family fortunes. Other books by the same author: *The New Treasure Seekers,* and *The Wouldbegoods,* being the further adventures of the treasure seekers. These stories need to be introduced to most children. Ages 8-12.

Snow Treasure. Marie McSwigan. Illustrated by Mary Reardon. Dutton. A group of Norwegian children manage to get blocks of gold out of Norway from right under the Nazis' noses, by fastening them to their sleds and coasting through the German camps. Based on a true story. Children from eight and up love this story. Ages 8-12.

Li Lun, Lad of Courage. Carolyn Treffinger. Illustrated by Kurt Wiese. Abingdon. A dramatic story of courage and endurance. Needs to be read aloud to be appreciated fully. All ages.

Twenty and Ten. Claire Huchet Bishop. Illustrated by by William Pene DuBois. Viking. The very moving and "suspenseful" story of twenty French children who hide ten Jewish children from the Nazis. Ages 8-12.

The Blue Cat of Castle Town. Catherine Coblentz. Illustrated by Janice Holland. Longmans. A blue kitten, born under a blue moon, and living near a small Vermont town in the time of the Revolutionary War, is the hero of this beautiful story. Ages 8-12.

The Wind in the Willows. Kenneth Grahame. Illustrated by Ernest Shepard. (There are many other attractive editions of this book. I happen to like this one with the black-and-white illustrations best.) Scribner. All ages.

The Reluctant Dragon. Kenneth Grahame. Illustrated by Ernest Shepard. Holiday. A delightful little book which contains the story of a dragon who writes poetry, and of the boy who knows all about dragons. When St. George appears to fight the dragon the boy is torn between wanting to see a fight and saving his friend the dragon. How he arranges to have the fight "thrown" and save all faces is very good. There is much more in this story than meets the eye. Ages 8-14.

To See the Queen. Katherine Gibson. Longmans. A story of Princess Isabella of France who married King Richard II of England when she was very young, and of the shepherd boy who went to see her. The princess ran away and was taken in by the boy's family. There she learned to be a *real* queen. Charming story. Ages 8-12.

The Matchlock Gun. Walter Edmonds. Illustrated by Paul Lanz. Dodd. When eleven-year-old Edward Alstyne's father went off to search for marauding Indians, Edward, with his mother's help, placed an old Spanish gun on a table aimed at the window, and thus was able to save his mother's life. A very dramatic story and needs to be read aloud to be fully appreciated. Ages 8-12.

The Cat Who Went to Heaven. Elizabeth Coatsworth. Illustrated by Lynd Ward. Macmillan. Newbery Medals book. A three-colored cat came into the home of a Japanese artist and brought him good luck. A beautiful story. This also needs to be read aloud and shared. Ages 8-12.

Blind Colt. Written and illustrated by Glen Rounds. Holiday. Whitey adopts and trains a blind colt. A warm, lovely story of an unforgettable horse and a boy's love for it. Short. Best appreciated read aloud. Ages 8-12.

Tales from Silver Lands. Charles Finger. Illustrated by Paul Honoré. Doubleday. Legendary stories of South American Indians. Too difficult for children to read at the age they can enjoy them. Ages 10-14.

Shen of the Sea. Arthur Chrisman. Illustrated by Elsie Hasselriis. Dutton. Short stories about Chinese people. They have a folklore quality and explain the whys of many things in a very amusing fantastic way, gunpowder, chopsticks, tea, printing, etc. Beautifully told. Difficult for children to read but they enjoy hearing them. Two of the most popular with children from nine years up are "Four Generals," and "Pies for a Princess." Grownups will love them too. Ages 8-14.

The Peterkin Papers. Lucretia Hale. Illustrated by Harold Brett. Houghton. Twenty-two stories about the stupid Peterkin family who get into all kinds of trouble but are helped by The Lady from Philadelphia. Especially good for family reading, as the youngest will enjoy it as much as the oldest. Ages 8-12.

Call it Courage. Written and illustrated by Armstrong Sperry. Macmillan. A Newbery Medal book. Mafatu, son of a chief on a Polynesian island, feared the sea. He went off in his canoe to prove his courage, taking only his dog. He encountered storm, savages, loneliness, sharks. His struggle to live, to make a boat for his return, his killing of the shark, all make a really tremendous story that children of ten and up love to hear. Based on a Polynesian legend. Ages 10-16.

The King of the Golden River. John Ruskin. With pictures by Mary Lott. Seaman. Macmillan. The cruel Black Brothers lost their inheritance because they were cruel, but it was regained by love. A classic fairy tale that children enjoy. Ages 8-12.

The Bird's Christmas Carol. Kate Douglas Wiggin. Illustrated by Jessie Gillespie. Houghton. How Carol Bird made Christmas for the Ruggleses who lived in the rear. The best part of this story, of course, is about the Ruggleses and their mother's training them for the Christmas dinner at Carol's. If you know the story you can tell the first part and read only the funny part about the Ruggleses. The end is sad but, of course, children are noted for liking to weep over stories. The trouble is, you may weep yourself when you read it. Ages 8-12.

Uncle Remus. Joel Chandler Harris. Illustrated by A. B. Frost. Appleton. Thirty-four legends of the old plantation as told by an old Negro, Uncle Remus. Brer Rabbit plays astonishing pranks and outwits his stronger neighbors. Dialect is difficult for children to read but it is good for reading aloud if *you* can read dialect. A little Negro boy once asked me, "Do you have this here book written in English? My mother says she can't read it." Ages 6-12.

The Children's Homer. Padraic Colum. Illustrated by Willy Pogany. Macmillan. A wonderful telling of the Odyssey and The Iliad for young people. Unless it is read aloud only the unusual child will read it for himself. Ages 10-16.

The Sampo: Hero adventures from the Finnish Kalevala. James Baldwin. Illustrated by N. C. Wyeth. Scribner. A great body of Finnish folklore is called the Kalevala, originally an epic poem. Here is the full telling of the story, concerning the great heroes of Finland, the forging of the magic mill, the sampo, and the adventures of the heroes when they tried to get it back. A really thrilling story for young and old. Ages 10-16.

White Stag. Written and illustrated by Kate Seredy. Viking. Newbery Medal book. Hero tale of the legendary founding of Hungary when the twins, Hunor and Magyar, and Bendeguz and finally his son, Attilla, led their peoples to their promised land, guided at times by the white stag and the red eagle. Beautiful to look at and a beautiful story to hear. Not long. Ages 10-16.

Railroad to Freedom. Hildegarde Hoyt Swift. Illstrated by James Daugherty. Harcourt. The story of Harriet Tubman, the Negro girl who escaped from slavery and then brought more than three hundred of her people to the North by the Underground Railway. Very dramatic. Ages 12-16.

Amos Fortune, Free Man. Elizabeth Yates. Illustrated by Nora Unwin. Aladdin Books. A prince, born free in Africa, was sold as a slave in America. Eventually he bought his own freedom and became a free man, married, lived in Jaffrey, New Hampshire. When he died he left a small sum of money for the school. A lovely warm story, and true. Very much liked by children. Isn't it wonderful that children like good stories like this? Ages 10-16.

Bob, Son of Battle. Alfred Ollivant. Grosset. A great dog story, being the life of Old Bob, champion sheep dog, and of his rival, Red Wull, and Red Wull's rascally master. Written in dialect which is hard for children to read. A dramatic enough story to stand reading aloud to many ages of children and grownups. Ages 10-16.

Freddy Goes to Florida. Walter Brooks. Illustrated by Kurt Wiese. Knopf. Children of eight or more can read this easily themselves, but younger children like it, and it is a good book to read to a mixed group. Ages 6-12.

Mr. Popper's Penguins. Florence and Richard Atwater. Illustrated by Robert Lawson. Little. Another book children will read themselves, but they enjoy hearing it. Funny things are always nice to share. Mr. Popper, a house painter, is an Arctic enthusiast. Commodore Drake sends him a penguin. The troubles and the fun for Mr. Popper and for us, too, begin then. Ages 6-12.

Homer Price. Written and illustrated by Robert McCloskey. Viking. Six short stories about the highly original Homer. The great favorite is the one about the doughnut machine. Ages 6-12.

All-Of-A-Kind Family. Sidney Taylor. Illustrated by Helen John. Wilcox. Five little Jewish girls grow up in New York's Lower East Side in a happy home atmosphere. Delightful picture of a Jewish family. Ages 8-12.

Once the Hodja. Alice Geer Kelsey. Illustrated by Frank

Dobias. Longmans. Terribly funny Turkish tales about that character, Nasr-ed-Din Hodja, who gets into trouble and gets out of it again. The stories are quite short. Ages 10-16.

The Jungle Book. Rudyard Kipling. Illustrated by Kurt Wiese. Doubleday. Stories of the jungle life of Mowgli who was adopted by a wolf pack and taught the laws of the jungle. Also contains that very wonderful story "Rikki Tikki Tavi" that every child should know. Will be liked by everyone from eight years up.

Steppin and Family. Hope Newell. Pictures by Anne Merriman Peck. Oxford. Steppin, a boy of Harlem, wanted to be a tap dancer. He found it took a lot of hard work. A story that children like a great deal because the people in it seem so real. Ages 10-14.

Otto of the Silver Hand. Written and illustrated by Howard Pyle. Scribner. A tale of the olden days when robber barons preyed upon the country. Otto was kidnapped by them. Beautifully told. Ages 10-14.

Smoky the Cow Horse. Written and illustrated by Will James. Scribner. A Newbery Medal book. The life story of a cow pony as seen from his eyes, telling of roundups, rodeos, the corral and range. Ages 8-12.

The Merry Adventures of Robin Hood. Written and illustrated by Howard Pyle. Scribner. This is considered the best-written of all the Robin Hoods. It is too difficult for a youngster below Junior High level to read to himself but he enjoys hearing it. Ages 12-16.

The Story of King Arthur and His Knights. Written and illustrated by Howard Pyle. Scribner. Beautifully told stories of the Knights of the Round Table. Ages 12-16.

Treasure Island. Robert Louis Stevenson. Many editions. One of the first real adventure stories children will listen to. If read to an eight- or nine-year-old he will reread it for himself later.

Back to Treasure Island by Harold A. Calahan. Vanguard.

Is a good followup. Same characters and same style of writing. Ages 8-16.

Ol' Paul the Mighty Logger. Written and illustrated by Glen Rounds. Holiday. One of the funniest and most popular of the Old Paul books. Ages 10-16.

Chucklebait: Funny stories for everyone. Selected by Margaret Scoggin. Knopf. Many funny stories that have been found tried and true with young people. Guaranteed to make them laugh. Ages 12-16.

Holiday stories good to read aloud or to oneself:

Christmas

A Visit from St. Nicholas. Clement C. Moore. In many editions. The favorite story for all children.

Paddy's Christmas. Helen Monsell. Illustrated by Kurt Wiese. Knopf. Little children just love this story about Paddy, the bear cub who wanted to know what Christmas was. Ages 3-8.

Christmas Whale. Written and illustrated by Roger Duvoisin. Knopf. Another great favorite. A picture book telling what Santa Claus did when his reindeer became ill. Ages 3-8.

Lullaby. Josephine Bernhard. Illustrated by Irena Lorentowicz. Roy. Why the pussy cat washes himself so often. A folk tale adapted from the Polish. A beautiful book liked by little children. Ages 3-8.

Noël for Jeanne Marie. Francoise Seignobosc. Scribner. A charming book, telling how Jeanne Marie, a little French girl, let her sheep share in the Christmas. Brief text. Ages 3-8.

Told Under the Christmas Tree. Selections by the Literature Committee of the Association for Childhood Education. Illustrated by Maud and Miska Petersham. Macmillan. Contains many familiar stories and some not so well known. Some are complete stories and some are taken from books. A good collection to have on hand. Ages 8-12.

This Way to Christmas. Ruth Sawyer. With illustrations

in color by Maginel Wright Barney. Harper. Stories within a story told to a little boy who was in the country and lonesome. People of different nationalities tell him stories from their homelands. The stories themselves are better than the framework. These stories are the best Christmas stories I know. "The Voyage of the Wee Red Cap" is a great favorite with all ages. "The Animals' Christmas" and "The Christmas That was Almost Lost" are favorites with little children. The loveliest of all is "Gifts for a First Birthday," a gypsy story. This book is to be owned and used every Christmas. Ages 5-12.

Torten's Christmas Secret. Maurice Dolbier. Illustrated by Robert Henneberger. Little. How Santa and one of his helpers managed to take care of all the bad little boys and girls. Ages 6-9.

Kersti and St. Nicholas. Written and illustrated by Hilda Van Stockum. Viking. A beautiful book that amuses children very much because Kersti, a naughty little girl, goes out to meet St. Nicholas and persuades him to give presents to naughty children. Ages 7-12.

Once in the Year. A Christmas Story. Elizabeth Yates. Illustrated by Nora S. Unwin. Coward. A retelling of two old Christmas legends of the flowering forest and the animals talking at midnight. A little boy sees and hears it all. Very moving and beautiful. Ages 8-12.

A Tree for Peter. Written and illustrated by Kate Seredy. Viking. A Christmas that came to a little lame boy in shanty town. A sentimental story that children love. Ages 9-12.

The Light at Tern Rock. Julia Sauer. Illustrated by Georges Schreiber. Viking. A boy and his mother go out to spend just two weeks at the lighthouse on Tern Rock and to be home in time for Christmas. It soon becomes apparent that the lighthouse keeper had no intention of coming back. The effect on the boy and the eventual good Christmas is a lovely story. Ages 9-12.

In Clean Hay. Eric Kelley. Illustrated by Maud and Miska

Petersham. Macmillan. Two children who went to the city on Christmas Eve to give their puppet show and were disappointed when their show was interrupted. Describes a wonderful experience of giving. A Polish story. Ages 9-12.

Maggie Rose: The Birthday Christmas. Ruth Sawyer. Pictures by Maurice Sendak. Harper. A little Maine girl sells berries to get money for a Christmas celebration for her shiftless family, and to repay some of the nice things that have been done for them by neighbors. The effect on the family is terrific. A lovely story and children adore it. It can be read before Christmas time ending at Christmas, which is where the story itself ends. Ages 9-12.

The Bird's Christmas Carol. Kate Douglas Wiggin. Illustrated by Jessie Gillespie. Houghton. Ages 5-12.

Tono Antonio. Ruth Sawyer. Viking. A modern Spanish story of a boy who takes his father's place in taking the goats to the city to sell milk to sailors. How he entertains the people at the hotel and brings money and presents home, together with his adventures on the way, makes a wonderful Christmas story that is different. Needs to be read aloud to children to be appreciated. Ages 10-14.

Why the Chimes Rang. Raymond Alden. With illustrations by Evelyn Copeland. Bobbs. An old story but, as the bookseller said, "The children are new." Ages 8-12.

A Christmas Carol. Charles Dickens. Story for Christmas. Illustrated by Robert Hall. Macmillan. No Christmas list would be complete without this story which every family should have and read once a year. Ages 8 and up.

Saint Santa Claus. Ruth Rounds. Dutton. A modern miracle in which an American boy and a little girl are saved from an airplane crash in the Alps by a monk who lived five centuries before. The fantasy is very real to the children. It is a true miracle. Ages 9-12.

Merry Christmas to You. Stories for Christmas. Compiled by Wilhelmina Harper. Illustrated by Wilfred Jones. Dutton.

A collection of stories for the 9s-12s. Includes many familiar ones.

Long Christmas. Ruth Sawyer. Illustrated by Valenti Angelo. Viking. One of our greatest storytellers has told some magnificent Christmas stories from little-known legends. Ages 10-14.

Fireside Book of Yuletide Tales. Edited by Edward C. Wagenknecht. Illustrated by Warren Chappell. Bobbs. A huge collection of Christmas tales for the whole family. Should be on every family shelf. All ages.

Thanksgiving

Harvest Feast: Stories of Thanksgiving Yesterday and Today. Compiled by Wilhelmina Harper. Illustrated by Wilfred Jones. Dutton. One of the few collections of Thanksgiving stories. Contains the best story for little children "Old Man Rabbit's Thanksgiving Dinner," which can be found nowhere else. Ages 8-12.

The Thanksgiving Story. Alice Dalgliesh. Illustrated by Scribners. The real story of the beginning of Thanksgiving put into a beautiful book and beautifully told. Ages 6-12.

Hallowe'en

Spooks and Spirits and Shadowy Shapes. Aladdin Books. Modern spooky stories for little children to read for themselves. It is very popular with little children partly because there isn't too much for them to read for Hallowe'en. The stories are by excellent authors. Ages 8-10.

Giants and Witches, and a Dragon or Two. Selected by Phyllis Fenner. Illustrated by Henry Pitz. Knopf. Anything with a witch or giant or cat serves for Hallowe'en with the very little. These are old favorites. "Hansel & Gretel" etc. Ages 8-12.

Ghosts and Goblins. Compiled by Wilhelmina Harper. Illustrated by Wilfred Funk. Dutton. A good collection of ghosty tales from many sources and of many kinds. Ages 8-12.

Spooks of the Valley. Louis C. Jones. Houghton. Excellent and popular ghost stories of New York State. Ages 10-14.

Ghosts, Ghosts, Ghosts. Selected by Phyllis Fenner. Illustrated by Manning deV. Lee. Watts. A fine collection of ghost stories from many sources. Very popular with children. Ages 10-16.

The Legend of Sleepy Hollow. Washington Irving. In many editions. Still a favorite for Hallowe'en. Ages 12-16.

Easter

Miss Flora McWhimsey's Easter Bonnet. Marian Foster. Lothrop. Miss Flora, Diana's favorite doll, who did not have a new bonnet to wear to the Easter party, and Peterkins the rabbit, who supplied one for her. Ages 5-6.

Country Bunny and the Little Gold Shoes, as told to Jennifer. By DuBose Heyward. Pictures by Marjorie Flack. Houghton. How a little country rabbit wanted to be an Easter Bunny and how she managed it. One of the few stories about Easter for little children. A great favorite. Ages 5-7.

The Egg Tree. Story and pictures by Katherine Milhous. Scribner. A beautiful picture book showing the children how to make a decorated Easter Egg, and all the neighbors coming to see it. Ages 6-8.

Holiday Roundup. Lucile Pannell and Frances Cavanah. Illustrated by Manning deV. Lee. Macrae. A collection of fifty-two stories about twenty-seven national, religious and sentimental holidays. One of the few collections that contains Jewish festivals. Ages 10-16.

XVII

"The habit of owning books."

BOOKS FOR A HOME LIBRARY

MANY OF US would like to start libraries for our children and build them up through the years. We want books that children will enjoy reading and rereading, and keep for their own children. There are book lists and book lists. Actually, of course, the only kind of list of much value is one for each individual child. That is impossible here. The next best thing is a list of books that, as nearly as possible, all children will like.

Several years ago, during the height of the Great Books furor, when a hundred books from all times were suggested as basic reading for adults, eighteen librarians from all parts of the country were asked to make a similar list of fifty books for children. It was to be the nucleus for a home library, a starting point. The choices were based on two points only: literary quality and children's own likes. For after all, said these librarians, why select a book, no matter how good we think it is, if no one will read it? So the books on the list were to be tested books, old and new.

It was not an easy job to select only fifty. There were disagreements, of course. But when the librarians had finished, and saw those fifty books on the table in front of them, they were rather proud of their choice. It did not mean that there were only fifty good children's books in the world but these were fifty, as near as they could determine, that children should not miss. They put in an anthology of poetry and prose to provide specimens of additional works, such as *The Peterkin Papers, The Travels of Baron Munchausen, The Arabian Nights* and *Grimm's Fairy Tales.*

The alternatives are titles that did not get quite enough votes for the main list. After all, they were human, these librarians, and had their favorites.

Since that meeting, to be sure, wonderful books have been published, many of them worthy of this list. But the original list still looks like one of the best starting points for a child's library. Whether you agree about individual titles or not, anyone must say that every book on it is good and worthy to be in a child's life. Remember, it is only a starting point. Each individual child will have other favorites to add.

Here, then, is a list of one hundred books (fifty first choices and fifty alternates) to start you off building your child's library.

For the youngest

The Story of Little Black Sambo (original edition). Helen Bannerman. Lippincott.

Pelle's New Suit. Elsa Beskow. Harper.

A Ring o' Roses. Leslie Brooke. Warne.

Mike Mulligan and His Steam Shovel. Virginia Burton. Houghton.

The Hey Diddle Diddle Picture Book and *Picture Book, No. 2.* Randolph Caldecott. Warne.

The Story About Ping. Marjorie Flack. Viking.

Millions of Cats. Wanda Gag. Coward.

And To Think That I Saw It On Mulberry Street. Dr. Seuss. Vanguard.

Make Way for Ducklings. Robert McCloskey. Viking.

The Tale of Peter Rabbit. Beatrix Potter. Warne (original edition only).

Alternates:

Little Tim and the Brave Sea Captain. Edward Ardizzone. Oxford.

Don't Count Your Chicks. Ingri and Edgar d'Aulaire. Doubleday.

Madeline. Ludwig Bemelmans. Simon & Schuster.

The Five Chinese Brothers. Claire Huchet Bishop. Coward.

Johnny Crow's Garden. Leslie Brooke. Warne.

In the Forest. Marie Ets. Viking.

ABC Bunny. Wanda Gag. Coward.

Little Toot. Hardi Gramatky. Putnam.

Under the Window. Kate Greenaway. Warne.

Curious George. H. R. Rey. Houghton.

For the "middle-aged" group

Fairy Tales. Hans Andersen. Translated by Jean Hersholt. Heritage.

Leif the Lucky. Ingri and Edgar d'Aulaire. Doubleday.

Alice's Adventures in Wonderland and *Through the Looking Glass.* Lewis Carroll. With Tenniel illustrations. Macmillan.

Andy and the Lion. James Daugherty. Viking.

The Moffats. Eleanor Estes. Harcourt.

The Wind in the Willows. Kenneth Grahame. Scribner.

The Just So Stories. Rudyard Kipling. Doubleday.

The Blue Fairy Book. Andrew Lang. Longmans.

The Story of Doctor Dolittle. Hugh Lofting. Lippincott.

The Adventures of Pinocchio. Carl Lorenzini. Macmillan.

A Pocketful of Rhymes. Katherine Lovelace. Crowell.

Winnie the Pooh. A. A. Milne. Dutton.

Floating Island. Ann Parrish. Harper.

The Good Master. Kate Seredy. Viking.

Heidi. Johanna Spyri. Lippincott.

Honk the Moose. Phil Stong. Dodd.

Mary Poppins. P. L. Travers. Reynal.

The Little House in the Big Woods and *Little House on the*

Prairie. Laura Ingalls Wilder. Harper.
The Swiss Family Robinson. Johann Wyss. Macmillan.

Alternates:

Mr. Popper's Penguins. Richard and Florence Atwater. Little.
The Story of the Treasure Seekers. Edith Bland. Coward.
Joan of Arc. Boutet de Monvel. Century.
Caddie Woodlawn. Carol Ryrie Brink. Macmillan.
Down, Down the Mountain. Ellis Credle. Nelson.
Paddle to the Sea. Holling C. Holling. Houghton.
Little Pear. Eleanor Lattimore. Harcourt.
The Complete Nonsense Book. Edward Lear. Dodd.
Homer Price. Robert McCloskey. Viking.
The Ship's Parrot. Honoré Morrow. Morrow.

For older boys and girls

Little Women. Louisa May Alcott. Little.
The Adventures of Tom Sawyer. Samuel L. Clemens. Harper.
The Prince and the Pauper. Samuel L. Clemens. Harper.
The Adventures of Robinson Crusoe. Daniel Defoe. Houghton.
Johnny Tremain. Esther Forbes. Houghton.
Smoky. Will James. Scribner.
The Jungle Book. Rudyard Kipling. Doubleday.
The Boys' King Arthur. Ed. by Lanier. Scribner.
Jim Davis. John Masefield. McKay.
On to Oregon. Honoré Morrow. Morrow.
A Mythology.
A Poetry Anthology.
A Prose Anthology.
Men of Iron. Howard Pyle. Harper.
The Merry Adventures of Robin Hood. Howard Pyle. Scribner.
Bright Island. Mabel Island. Random House.
Abe Lincoln Grows Up. Carl Sandburg. Harcourt.
Call It Courage. Armstrong Sperry. Macmillan.

Treasure Island. Robert Louis Stevenson. Scribner.
The Story of Mankind. Hendrik Van Loon. Liveright.

Alternates:

The Deerslayer. James Fenimore Cooper. Scribner.
Daniel Boone. James Daugherty. Viking.
David Copperfield. Charles Dickens. Dodd.
Jock of Bushveld. Sir James Fitzpatrick. Longmans.
Downright Dencey. Caroline D. Snedeker. Doubleday.
Mysterious Island. Jules Verne. Scribner.
On Safari. Theodore Waldeck. Viking.

XVIII

"Keep your sap running."

THE THREE E'S

GROWNUPS ARE OFTEN a little shy about children's books. They do not know what to ask for. This book you are reading may help some. But to really find the book that does for a child what we want it to, we should have what I like to call the 3 E's—Education, Experience, and Enthusiasm.

By Education I do not mean going to school. What I really mean is an *awareness* of children's books. We can't get along with the books we knew as children, to give to our own children now, any more than we can remember what we ate and just feed our own children the same. Diet has changed. So have books. To be aware of new books coming all the time, and new editions of old books, we ourselves must read—not necessarily the children's books themselves, there are too many for that, but read *about* them. There are excellent reviews of them in every Sunday book section, and almost all of the women's magazines review children's books once in a while, as do many other magazines. The thing to remember is that books for children that are reviewed are *good* books, or the ones the reviewers have thought were good. With so many books coming out each year, the reviewers could not possibly review them all, so they do not waste time telling us about those they do not like. Many good books are not reviewed but the outstanding books are. Every year the

Book Week and Book Festival Week book pages carry many reviews. Book Week comes about the second week in November and Book Festival Week comes in May. Prizes are awarded to books considered a contribution to children's literature.

An award called the Newbery Medal is given in the early spring for the best book of the previous year as judged by librarians throughout the country. This does not necessarily mean that it is the most popular book with children, but it has been thought to be of high literary quality. A Caldecott medal is given for the outstanding picture book. If you have been keeping up on children's book news you will surely see the announcement of the prizes and make note of the books in your mind.

The fact that a book is good doesn't mean that every child will like it. We know a good deal about what our own children like, but we must also give our children every opportunity to see books at bookshops, book exhibits, the public library. Like everything else in the world, if reading is worth anything it is worth making an effort for, and we should put our minds to it. Get acquainted with the children's books as they come out each year, by review or by actual sight of them.

Experience. We must have a little interest in what our children are reading. You should discuss books, read aloud to the children, let them read to you. Buy books. Let them buy books. If you live in a town with a good bookshop, or in your travels visit a city where there is one, turn the children loose in it for a while. Give them time. Let them browse. "Browse" is a wonderful word. It actually means "to nibble." Let the children nibble here and nibble there until they find something that tastes good to them. Let them choose what they want and let them pay for it. It will be invaluable experience for the children. They will be learning how to be canny, thoughtful buyers. If they make mistakes, these are not too serious. Nothing means quite so much as what we've chosen for ourselves. All this is experience plus the value of the books themselves.

If there is no bookshop there surely is a public library. Let them borrow books. See that they have cards to the public library. And let them select for themselves. Share in the joy of selection, if you will, but let them have the final say.

The greatest thing of all is Enthusiasm. We can't force it if we really don't have it, but who knows how much enthusiasm we might have if we tried?

This book is able to tell you only a few of all the good books in the world that children like. There are other sources of help:

Periodical sources

The Book Sections of newspapers. Already mentioned.

The Book Sections of magazines.

The Children's Catalog. H. W. Wilson Co.

Every public and school library will have this invaluable book. The librarians are pleased to have people look at it. It is a selected list, and does not include all of the good books, but it is very useful. The books are listed by title, author, subject. There is a brief description of each book under the author's name, together with price, publisher, and school grade at which the child might be interested. The grade is only a suggestion, and usually covers quite a range of years. At the back is a list of books suitable for certain grades. There are periodic supplements that keep the catalogue up-to-date. When in doubt as to what to give a child for his birthday or Christmas, consult *The Children's Catalog.* Remember, "the books may be old but the child is new."

Recommended Children's Books: As professionally evaluated by librarians for librarians in Library Journal. Editor, Louise Davis. A yearly list taken from reviews in *The Library Journal,* 62 W. 45th St., New York 36.

Books about books that will help your enthusiasm:

First Adventures in Reading. May Lamberton Becker. Lippincott. The development of a child's reading taste from nursery rhymes to mystery tales. Written from the point of view of the intelligent mother interested in guiding her child's reading. A charming conversational style of writing.

Adventures in Reading. May Lamberton Becker. Lippincott. Friendly informal talks on books and reading full of the author's enthusiasm for her subject. Book lists at the end of chapters. For older children than the book listed before.

Bequest of Wings. Annis Duff. Viking. A family's pleasure with books. The intimate reading experiences shared by two children and their parents. Picture books, poetry, all kinds of books, are discussed.

Longer Flight. Annis Duff. Viking. A discussion of the books these same children read as they grow older. One feels that the parents grow in understanding too.

Reading With Children. Anne Thaxter Eaton. Viking. A very wise and stimulating account of the experiences this warm, enthusiastic librarian had introducing books to children. Book lists at end of each chapter.

Treasure for the Taking. A Book List for Boys and Girls. Anne Thaxter Eaton. Viking. An annotated list of books for boys and girls from the first picture books through high school age, arranged according to subject. A very carefully selected list.

Our Library: The Story of a School Library That Works. Phyllis Fenner. John Day. What a school library can and did do in bringing children and books together. Anecdotes and experiences of a librarian, with many book titles.

The Right Book for the Right Child. Graded buying list of children's books. Day. Selected and annotated by a committee of The American Library Association under chairmanship of Miriam Snow. A very readable and useful book fulfilling its title.

Gateways to Readable Books. An annotated graded list of books in many fields for adolescents who find reading difficult. Ruth Strang. H. W. Wilson. More than 700 titles suggested for children whose reading ability falls below the level expected of pupils in high-school grades. Suggestions for arousing reading interest.

Your Child's Reading Today. Josette Frank. Doubleday. A discussion of books for today's children. It includes an appraisal of the effects of TV, the comics and radio on the child's reading, and book lists arranged in categories.

A Selected List of Books for Boys and Girls. May be obtained from The Children's Book Council, 62 W. 45th St., New York 19.

In that charming book *Miss Hickory* by Carolyn S. Bailey, when the doll with a hickory-nut head and an apple-tree twig for a body is left to face the cold winter alone, the old crow says to her something like this, "Cheer up, Miss Hickory, spring will come again. But there is one thing you must remember. Keep your sap running." If we grownups would do our best by our children in bringing them to books, the kind of books they enjoy, we must keep on our toes, keep up with the books, and *keep our sap running.*

Imagination and Children's Literature

BY PADRAIC COLUM

There is no time in one's life when right reading is so important as in one's childhood: one has good instincts then; later on they become corrupted by continuous reading of that which is just current and topical. The good instincts that the child has, and the taste that goes with them, should be kept right. But we spoil them. We spoil them by giving children snippets out of newspapers and stories which, because the writers have to follow a certain vein year in, year out, are trite—trite in invention and trite in expression.

When I say that children have good instincts in reading I mean that they respond to real imagination when it is shown in a story. Now, what is imagination? It is not merely a faculty for stringing improbabilities together and making up a world that is wholly unreal. *Imagination is the faculty of revealing things freshly and surprisingly.*

Sometime, perhaps very soon, it will come to be recognized that it is as important to cultivate the imagination as it is to cutivate the will or the intelligence. At present our systems of education are directed towards training the will or training the intelligence, but perhaps the time is at hand when we will have an education that will be directed towards training the intelligence and the will through the imagination. For

Reprinted by permission from *Child Life,* November, 1935.

imagination is one of our great faculties: it is the one quality common to all great men—to soldiers and statesmen, to saints and artists, to scientists, philosophers and great businessmen. Says the Serpent to Eve in "Back to Methuselah," "She told it to me as a marvelous story of something that never happened to a Lillith that never was. She did not know that imagination is the beginning of creation. You imagine what you desire; you will what you imagine; and at last you create what you will." The time may come when that sentence will be written above all places of education: "Imagination is the beginning of creation. . . . You imagine what you desire; you will what you imagine; and at last you create what you will." If children are to will out of their imagination and create out of their will, we must see to it that their imaginations are not clipped and made trivial.

A great writer, Sir Walter Scott, has written down all that is to be said as to the way stories for children should be told. "A good thought has come into my head," he writes in his *Journal for 1827*, "to write stories for little Johnnie Lockhart from the *History of Scotland*, like those taken from the *History of England*. I will not write mine quite as simply as Croker has done. I am persuaded both children and the lower class of readers hate books which are written down to their capacity, and love those that are more composed for their elders and betters. I will make, if possible, a book that a child will understand, yet a man will feel some temptation to peruse should he chance to take it up. It will require, however, a simplicity of style not quite my own. The grand and interesting consists in ideas, not words."

Scott, I am certain, was right in what he puts down here. Children are quick to feel patronage. The story-teller must have a respect for the child's mind and the child's conception of the world, knowing it for a complete mind and a complete conception. Scott had that kind of a respect; Hans Andersen, Stevenson, Kipling had it, and their ever memorable stories are grounded on it.

It is more important, I believe, to let the child's imagination develop than it is to labour to inculcate in him or her some correct ethical point of view. If a child has in his or her mind the images that imaginative literature can communicate—the heroic, sweet or loving types that are in the world's great stories—it is much more likely that he or she will grow up into a fine human being than if some austere mentor spoke to them out of every page of their reading. I think the mood of a child's story should be one of kindliness. I do not mean that the characters in a story should be always kind to each other. I mean that the auditor or the reader should be assured that the teller is inspired with a mood of kindliness for his conspicuous character. "Now you must know that the King had no horse to give Boots but an old broken-down jade," says the Norse story, "for his six other sons had carried off all the horses; but Boots did not care a pin for that; he sprang up on his sorry old steed. 'Farewell, father,' said he; 'I'll come back, next year, and like enough I shall bring my six brothers with me'; and with that he rode off." When we hear this we know that the teller of the tale has the right feeling for his hero.

With the mood of kindliness there should be the mood of adventure. The hero should be one who is willing to take strange paths in the morning and lie down under the giant's roof when darkness falls. "After that they went around the castle, and at last they came to a great hall where the Troll's two great swords hung high up on the wall. 'I wonder if you are man enough to wield one of these,' said the Princess. 'Who? I?' said the lad; 'twould be a pretty thing indeed if I couldn't wield one of these.' With that he put two or three chairs one a-top of the other, jumped up, and touched the biggest sword with his finger tips, tossed it up in the air, and caught it again by the hilt; leapt down, and at the same time dealt such a blow with it on the floor that the whole hall shook." That is the humor proper to a hero.

Then there should be happenings in a child's story, many

happenings, even the same happenings over again. The good characters should undoubtedly be fine and upright, but we should not insist upon their being always good boys at school. If they are heroic and adventurous and have a simple-minded goodness it is enough; the stories they figure in need not bristle with moralities and recommendations to good conduct. And the old figures of romance should be left to the children: when Kings, Queens, and Princes have taken their leave of the political world they should still be left to flourish in the world of the child's romance. Witches, giants, dwarfs, gnomes and trolls should be left to them, too.

I think the ideal children's book should be, not a collection of stories, but a continuous narrative with the same characters living through many varied incidents. Things need not be too simplified in that world. It will be no harm if things are left mysterious there—such mysterious things are "magic," and "magic" is an element that is not only accepted but is looked for. And it flatters a child to be able to read a long story that has mysteries in it. *The probabilities that we know of from experience have no place in the world we make for a child.* A tree may talk; a swan may change into a king's daughter; a castle may be built up in an instant. We know tree, swan, and castle by their limitations, but a child knows them in their boundless possibilities. To a child each thing mentioned is distinct, unique, a thing in itself, having all the possibilities of things in Eden. Did we know, in the time that we flew kites, that there was a space in the atmosphere that no kite ever flew before and that our kite might enter it? That sense of boundless possibility should belong to everything in a child's story.

The delight in things, the sense of the uniqueness of things, is in every story that children delight in. An old lamp may be Aladdin's. A key may open the door to mystery. A dish may be the supreme possession of a king. *For children feel, as people with few possessions feel, the adventure and the enchantment that are in things.*

The Wingèd Horse

An Essay on the Art of Reading

BY HENRY BARNES

"Yes, there he sat, on the back of the wingèd horse!

"But what a bound did Pegasus make, when, for the first time, he felt the weight of a mortal man upon his loins! A bound, indeed! Before he had time to draw a breath, Bellerophon found himself five hundred feet aloft, and still shooting upward, while the winged horse snorted and trembled with terror and anger. Upward he went, up, up, up, until he plunged into the cold misty bosom of a cloud, at which, only a little while before, Bellerophon had been gazing, and fancying it a very pleasant spot. Then again, out of the heart of the cloud, Pegasus shot down like a thunderbolt, as if he meant to dash both himself and his rider headlong against a rock. Then he went through about a thousand of the wildest caprioles that had ever been performed either by a bird or a horse."

Grandfather paused in his reading. The young boy let out a long breath and laughed out loud. What a ride! The old man read on and the boy's eyes shone as he soared in

Reprinted (in part) by permission from *Education as an Art,* bulletin of the Rudolph Steiner School Association, Vol, 11, No. 3, Autumn, 1950.

imagination on the back of the wingèd horse. His heart beat in rhythm with the powerful sweep of the language and his eyes followed each change of expression on his grandfather's face. He watched the old man's hands twist and flutter and dive as he illustrated how Pegasus soared and plunged on his wild flight.

The boy was just six years old and he was hearing for the first time Hawthorne's wonderful telling of the story of Pegasus and Bellerophon. He asked for the story many times again and often pored over the picture of the winged steed and his young master on the cover of the book.

At the time when he first heard this story, he had not yet entered the first grade, nor could he write his own name. The black printed marks on the white page were mysterious and enchanted forms to him, meaningless and uninteresting in themselves, but from which the grown-ups freed the magic pictures which captured his imagination. And this hidden art, the grown-ups called *reading.*

Each time the story was read aloud, the little boy entered into it as though he heard it for the first time. Pegasus became a familiar companion to him. He saw him rearing in the clouds and when the sunlight caught the gleaming silver wing of an airplane far up in the blue sky, he cried: "See, there's Pegasus!"

Four or five years later came the great moment when he again discovered this volume of Hawthorne's *Wonder Book* and curled up to read about his beloved Pegasus for the first time himself! And as he read, he once again waited with Bellerophon at the spring and saw Pegasus descend in gleaming spirals from the blue sky and alight on the green grass by the fountain. He did not see the o's and s's and b's which his eyes read, for he was far away on the slopes of Mount Helicon. Nowhere did the long words of Latin origin or the difficult Greek names impede his progress for they were already familiar to his ear and he skimmed over them now, tasting their foreign flavor along with the homely clover of the words he knew.

When had this boy first started to learn to read? It was not in his reading lessons, when he first struggled to spell out words, but when he listened to the stories which were told and read aloud to him, into which he entered with his whole being. For reading is an art—the art of entering with one's whole soul into an experience outside oneself. It is a gleaning of the sunlight hidden in the hard kernel of the word. In its widest meaning, reading is not bound to the printed page, for do we not speak of reading a map? Reading the stars? Reading a man's expression? Reading his mind? It is always an intuitive divining of a meaning which may express itself in as many different ways as there are forms of life; it is always an inner, creative process. The technique of reading the printed word is a specialized branch of the reading process and should no more be confused with it than the technique of raising and lowering the fingers should be confused with the art of a pianist. At a time when in educational circles the art of reading is so generally identified with its mechanics, it is well to remember that many profound minds have been slow readers, often learning to read very late. Many creative writers are poor spellers and some of the greatest "readers of life" would show up poorly on the current reading tests, designed to show "intelligence"!

A vast amount of research has been done on the technique of reading and there now exists such a literature on "reading" that one who conscientiously tries to master it all is not likely to have either the courage or the time to attempt to teach children to read, or to read anything interesting himself! Much valuable and important knowledge has been gained, but the essence of how we learn to read remains, I believe, a mystery. That is, it is a living process, like learning to swim or to play the violin, which can be grasped by doing it and can never be fully analyzed intellectually or reduced to merely mechanical principles. Every good swimming teacher knows that the key to success is to let the beginner discover that he cannot sink if he tries. Water is buoyant and the first thing is to establish this confidence and let the learner enjoy this friendly element. And so also in learning to read, the key to success is the love and enjoyment of the great stories and poems which are the element in which the reader swims. Before a printed reader is ever opened, we must have done everything in our power to strengthen the inner muscles of the imagination and to awaken a love and enthusiasm for the living literature which the child is to read.

Index

The italicized page numbers refer to books described in full; other titles briefly noted.